365 BIBLE PROMISES *for Busy Dads*

365 BIBLE PROMISES
for Busy Dads

KEN R. CANFIELD

Tyndale House Publishers, Inc.
Wheaton, Illinois

ISBN 0-8423-2502-6

Printed in the United States of America

03 02 01 00 99 98 97 96
 8   7   6   5   4   3

CONTENTS

A Wise Father . . .

➢ **It is a wise father that knows his own child.** William Shakespeare

➢ A wise father helps his children think through potential dangers.

➢ A wise father establishes meaningful traditions for his family.

➢ A wise father prepares his family for crisis.

➢ A wise father asks for feedback on his fathering.

➢ A wise father helps his children develop their talents.

➢ A wise father sets guidelines for his children's behavior.

➢ A wise father shares his perspective and seeks to understand the perspective of his children.

☐ 1 _____

For the Lord your God is a compassionate God; He will not fail you nor destroy you nor forget the covenant with your fathers which He swore to them. (Deuteronomy 4:31, NASB)

Passing on the Father's love
Make a bold commitment: This year I will be the father my children need.

☐ 2 _____

I will proclaim the decree of the Lord: He said to me, "You are my Son; today I have become your Father." (Psalm 2:7)

Vocalize your commitment to your children; tell them you're dedicated to them.

☐ 3 _____

You husbands likewise, live with your wives in an understanding way, as with a weaker vessel, since she is a woman; and grant her honor as a fellow heir of the grace of life, so that your prayers may not be hindered. (1 Peter 3:7, NASB)

Passing on the Father's love
Ask your wife what her biggest struggle is as a mother.

☐ 4 _____

When his brothers saw that their father loved [Joseph] more than any of them, they hated him and could not speak a kind word to him. (Genesis 37:4)

Passing on the Father's love
Reflect on whether or not you've been playing favorites among your children; reach out to the neglected one today.

☐ 5 _____

Love never fails. . . . Now we see but a poor reflection as in a mirror; then we shall see face to face. Now I know in part; then I shall know fully, even as I am fully known. And now these three remain:

faith, hope and love. But the greatest of these is love. (1 Corinthians 13:8, 12-13)

Passing on the Father's love
Face your kids. Look at each one and say, "Read my lips"; then mouth the words "I love you."

☐ 6 _____

Religion that God our Father accepts as pure and faultless is this: to look after orphans and widows in their distress and to keep oneself from being polluted by the world. (James 1:27)

Passing on the Father's love
Take your child to a nursing home to visit a relative or friend.

☐ 7 _____

The heavens declare the glory of God; the skies proclaim the work of his hands. Day after day they pour forth speech; night after night they display knowledge. There is no speech or language where their voice is not heard. Their voice goes out into all the earth, their words to the ends of the world. (Psalm 19:1-4)

Passing on the Father's love
Check out a book from the library on constellations. Take your children out-side, and help them find some in the night sky.

A STRONG FINISH: Children never have been very good at listening to their elders, but they have never failed to imitate them. James Baldwin

☐ 8 _____

David also said to Solomon his son, "Be strong and courageous, and do the work. Do not be afraid or discouraged, for the Lord God, my God, is with you. He will not fail you or forsake you until all the work for the service of the temple of the Lord is finished. (1 Chronicles 28:20)

Passing on the Father's love

When your teenage daughter breaks up with her boyfriend, take her out to a nice restaurant to let her know that there's a man in her life who will always love and accept her.

☐ 9 _____

From infancy you have known the holy
Scriptures, which are able to make you wise
for salvation through faith in Christ Jesus.
(2 Timothy 3:15)

Passing on the Father's love
**Read your kids a Bible story, and help
them visualize what was happening.**

☐ 10 _____

For, dear brothers, you have been given freedom: not freedom to do wrong, but freedom
to love and serve each other. For the whole
Law can be summed up in this one command:
"Love others as you love yourself." (Galatians
5:13-14, TLB)

Passing on the Father's love
**Don't let your wife be the sole taxi
driver; next time *you* drive the children
to their activities.**

☐ 11 _____

Teach these things and make sure everyone learns
them well. . . . Until I get there, read and explain
the Scriptures to the church; preach God's Word.
(1 Timothy 4:11, 13, TLB)

Passing on the Father's love
Read the Bible as a family tonight, taking

turns each reading a verse; then discuss
what you've read.

☐ 12 _____

I will utter hidden things, things from of old—
what we have heard and known, what our fathers
have told us. (Psalm 78:2-3)

Passing on the Father's love
**Tell your kids a story that your grand-
father told you.**

☐ 13 _____

And we urge you, brothers, warn those who
are idle, encourage the timid, help the weak,
be patient with everyone. (1 Thessalonians
5:14)

Passing on the Father's love
**Help your teenagers be responsible in
the use of the car by asking that they
wash it, fill the gas tank, or drive their
younger siblings somewhere.**

☐ 14 _____

Therefore encourage one another and build each
other up, just as in fact you are doing. (1 Thessalonians 5:11)

Passing on the Father's love
**Take your child's artwork to your office,
and hang it in a prominent place.**

A STRONG FINISH: Does your child have trouble expressing himself verbally? Encourage other ways of expression: music, crayon drawings, performing skits. Art can be more than entertainment.

☐ 15 _____

We who are strong ought to bear with the failings of the weak and not to please ourselves. Each of us should please his neighbor for his good, to build him up. (Romans 15:1-2)

Passing on the Father's love
Play catcher at a local ball diamond while your child pitches.

☐ 16 _____

Our fathers disciplined us for a little while as they thought best; but God disciplines us for our good, that we may share in his holiness. (Hebrews 12:10)

Passing on the Father's love

If you catch your child in some wrong action, help him take responsibility by walking him through the process of asking forgiveness and making any needed restitution.

☐ 17 _____

Follow my advice, my son; always keep it in mind and stick to it. Obey me and live! Guard my words as your most precious possession. (Proverbs 7:1-2, TLB)

Passing on the Father's love

Set appropriate curfews for your children. Extend the curfews as the children earn your trust.

☐ 18 _____

During the seven years of abundance the land produced plentifully. Joseph collected all the food produced in those seven years of abundance in Egypt and stored it in the cities. (Genesis 41:47-48)

Passing on the Father's love

Take your child down to the bank, and help her set up her first savings account or add to her existing account. (Feel free to help with the minimum deposit.)

☐ 19 _____

When a country is rebellious, it has many rulers,

but a man of understanding and knowledge maintains order. (Proverbs 28:2)

Passing on the Father's love

When your children invite friends over to play, ask them to inform their guests of the house rules, instead of doing it yourself.

☐ 20 _____

We have heard with our ears, O God; our fathers have told us what you did in their days, in days long ago. With your hand you drove out the nations and planted our fathers; you crushed the peoples and made our fathers flourish. (Psalm 44:1-2)

Passing on the Father's love

Seek out an older father, and ask him about the greatest struggle he has faced in his fathering and how he has handled it.

☐ 21 _____

But if a man does not know how to manage his own household, how will he take care of the church of God? (1 Timothy 3:5, NASB)

Passing on the Father's love

For practical encouragement in how you can get more involved with your kids, read *How to Be Your Daughter's Daddy* by Dan Bolin or *How to Be Your Little Man's Dad* by Dan Bolin and Ken Sutterfield (Piñon Press).

A STRONG FINISH: One of the most powerful motivating forces available to parents is praise.
Gary Smalley

☐ 22 _____

He . . . established the law . . . which he commanded our forefathers to teach their children, so the next generation would know them, even the children yet to be born, and they in turn would tell their children. (Psalm 78:5-6)

Passing on the Father's love
Memorize a saying or Scripture verse with your kids. Quote it to each other.

☐ 23 _____

"My son," the father said, "you are always with me, and everything I have is yours. But we had to celebrate and be glad, because this brother of yours was dead and is alive again; he was lost and is found." (Luke 15:31-32)

Passing on the Father's love
Talk about an extended family member who has had a tough life, and discuss ways to help him or her.

☐ 24 _____

If you refuse to discipline your son, it proves you don't love him; for if you love him, you will be prompt to punish him. (Proverbs 13:24, TLB)

Passing on the Father's love
Have a brainstorm session with your kids about what kinds of consequences are appropriate for what kinds of misbehavior.

☐ 25 _____

Where there is no revelation, the people cast off restraint. (Proverbs 29:18)

Passing on the Father's love
Ask your children what makes them proud about their country or what their concerns are about it. What vision and hope do they have for our nation?

☐ 26 _____

By wisdom a house is built, and through understanding it is established; through knowledge its rooms are filled with rare and beautiful treasures. (Proverbs 24:3-4)

Passing on the Father's love
Assist your child in rearranging her bedroom.

□ 27 _____

After all, children should not have to save up for their parents, but parents for their children. So I will very gladly spend for you everything I have and expend myself as well. (2 Corinthians 12:14-15)

Passing on the Father's love
Show your kids the family budget.

□ 28 _____

Love is patient, love is kind. . . . It is not rude, it is not self-seeking. (1 Corinthians 13:4-5)

Passing on the Father's love
Have a "Table Manners" night. Take your family to a nice restaurant, and have everyone practice their good manners.

A STRONG FINISH: The faithful father is hardworking. He has made a lifelong commitment to stay in touch with his kids, to press on through the complexities and difficulties, to focus on his children.

WEEK 5

☐ 29 _____

Charm is deceptive, and beauty is fleeting; but
a woman who fears the Lord is to be praised.
Give her the reward she has earned, and let
her works bring her praise at the city gate.
(Proverbs 31:30-31)

Passing on the Father's love
**Give your wife a day off by taking your
kids somewhere or watching them while
she goes out with her girlfriends.**

☐ 30 _____

Yet, O Lord, you are our Father. We are the clay,
you are the potter; we are all the work of your
hand. (Isaiah 64:8)

Passing on the Father's love
**Ask your child what she would like to be
when she grows up.**

☐ 31 _____

When I was a boy in my father's house, still tender,
. . . he taught me and said, "Lay hold of my words
with all your heart; keep my commands and you
will live." (Proverbs 4:3-4)

Passing on the Father's love
**Ask your child if he has ever seen some-
one who has used drugs, and then discuss the harmful effects of drug use.**

☐ 32 _____

But blessed is the man who trusts in the Lord,
whose confidence is in him. (Jeremiah 17:7)

Passing on the Father's love
**Find an easy-to-read book or story about
some hero of the faith, and read it with
your kids.**

☐ 33 _____

I pray for you constantly, asking God, the glorious
Father of our Lord Jesus Christ, to give you wis-

dom to see clearly and really understand who Christ is and all that he has done for you. I pray that your hearts will be flooded with light so that you can see something of the future he has called you to share. I want you to realize that God has been made rich because we who are Christ's have been given to him! I pray that you will begin to understand how incredibly great his power is to help those who believe him. (Ephesians 1:16-19, TLB)

Passing on the Father's love
Ask your child what kids in his school need prayer, and then remember to pray for them as a family. Pray for your child's relationship with these kids, too.

☐ 34 _____

Let us hold unswervingly to the hope we profess, for he who promised is faithful. And let us consider how we may spur one another on toward love and good deeds. (Hebrews 10:23-24)

Passing on the Father's love
Form or join a group of fathers who meet regularly to share encouragement, accountability, and fathering insight.

☐ 35 _____

Do not let any unwholesome talk come out of your mouths, but only what is helpful for building others up according to their needs, that it may benefit those who listen. (Ephesians 4:29)

Passing on the Father's love
Praise your child for something in front
of his or her friends.

**A STRONG FINISH: How can we help children
perceive life as an act of contribution rather than
an act of accumulation?** Gordon MacDonald

WEEK **6**

☐ 36 _____

You should make it clear that for a man to refuse to look after his own relations, especially those actually living in his house, is a denial of the faith he professes. (1 Timothy 5:8, PHILLIPS)

Passing on the Father's love

Go to your job or go job-seeking this morning encouraged that you are seeking to provide for your family and thus accomplishing an important part of your fathering role.

☐ 37 _____

For you have been my hope, O Sovereign Lord, my
confidence since my youth. From birth I have relied
on you; you brought me forth from my mother's
womb. I will ever praise you. (Psalm 71:5-6)

Passing on the Father's love
**Go to your children's musical or athletic
performances. Be their main cheerleader.**

☐ 38 _____

Sing to God, sing praise to his name, extol him
who rides on the clouds—his name is the Lord—
and rejoice before him. A father to the fatherless, a
defender of widows, is God in his holy dwelling.
God sets the lonely in families, he leads forth the
prisoners with singing. (Psalm 68:4-6)

Passing on the Father's love
**Take your family to help out a single
mother's family in a practical way. It
might be yard work, changing the oil in
her car, or taking her children on a hike.**

☐ 39 _____

But among you there must not be even a hint of sexual
immorality, or of any kind of impurity, or of greed,
because these are improper for God's holy people. Nor
should there be obscenity, foolish talk or coarse joking,
which are out of place. (Ephesians 5:3-4)

Passing on the Father's love
Tell your children a clean, funny joke or story.

☐ 40 _____

The sacrifices of God are a broken spirit; a broken and contrite heart, O God, you will not despise. (Psalm 51:17)

Passing on the Father's love
If you give up something for Lent, consider doing it as a family to support each other more effectively.

☐ 41 _____

See how very much our heavenly Father loves us, for he allows us to be called his children—think of it—and we really *are!* (1 John 3:1, TLB)

Passing on the Father's love
Tell your kids, "I love you," even if you have already said so once this year.

☐ 42 _____

Which of you, if his son asks for bread, will give him a stone? Or if he asks for a fish, will give him a snake? If you, then, though you are evil, know how to give good gifts to your children, how much more will your Father in heaven give good gifts to those who ask him! (Matthew 7:9-11)

Passing on the Father's love

Help your children sell items for their church, school, or club sales drive.

A STRONG FINISH: You were a kid once, with similar, though different, experiences. Your ability to bring back those feelings and memories accurately will help you understand more of what your child is going through.

☐ 43 _____

"The glory of this present house will be greater than the glory of the former house," says the Lord Almighty. "And in this place I will grant peace." (Haggai 2:9)

Passing on the Father's love
After church today, ask your kids what part of the service they enjoyed most.

☐ 44 _____

Discipline your son, for in that there is hope; do not be a willing party to his death. (Proverbs 19:18)

Passing on the Father's love
When you discipline your child, be sure to explain why his or her behavior was wrong or harmful.

☐ 45 _____

They will perish, but you remain; they will all wear out like a garment. . . . But you remain the same, and your years will never end. The children of your servants will live in your presence; their descendants will be established before you. (Psalm 102:26-28)

Passing on the Father's love
Have a discussion with your wife to decide whom you want to take care of your children in the event of both your deaths.

☐ 46 _____

I swear by myself, declares the Lord, that because you have done this and not withheld your son, your only son, I will surely bless you and make your descendants as numerous as the stars in the sky and as the sand on the seashore. (Genesis 22:16-17)

Passing on the Father's love
Tell your kids about your family history. When you get to *them,* describe how they'll carry on a great tradition.

☐ 47 _____

If you pay attention to these laws and are careful to
follow them, then the Lord your God will keep his
covenant of love with you, as he swore to your forefathers. He will love you and bless you and increase
your numbers. He will bless the fruit of your
womb, the crops of your land—your grain, new
wine and oil—the calves of your herds and the
lambs of your flocks in the land that he swore to
your forefathers to give you. (Deuteronomy 7:12-
13)

Passing on the Father's love
**At some point in your child's teenage
years, give him or her a ceremonial blessing similar to the custom found in the
Bible.**

☐ 48 _____

A cheerful look brings joy to the heart, and good
news gives health to the bones. (Proverbs 15:30)

Passing on the Father's love
**Give your kids a back rub; have them
give you one.**

☐ 49 _____

Every high priest is selected from among men and
is appointed to represent them in matters related
to God. . . . He is able to deal gently with those
who are ignorant and are going astray, since he himself is subject to weakness. (Hebrews 5:1-2)

Passing on the Father's love

The next time your kids catch you in an inconsistency, don't be afraid to admit you are wrong.

A STRONG FINISH: Many people use their imaginations to see their limitations: "Oh, I could never be Miss America." Instead, encourage your kids to use their imaginations to visualize their possibilities. Judson Swihart

☐ 50 _____

At that time the disciples came to Jesus and asked, "Who is the greatest in the kingdom of heaven?" He called a little child and had him stand among them. And he said: ". . . See that you do not look down on one of these little ones. For I tell you that their angels in heaven always see the face of my Father in heaven." (Matthew 18:1, 10)

Passing on the Father's love
Listen to your children practice their musical pieces. Be their first real live audience.

☐ 51 _____

Train a child in the way he should go, and
when he is old he will not turn from it.
(Proverbs 22:6)

> *Passing on the Father's love*
> **Plan a weekend with your high schooler
> to go visit colleges.**

☐ 52 _____

For you know that we dealt with each of you as a
father deals with his own children, encouraging,
comforting and urging you to live lives worthy of
God, who calls you into his kingdom and glory.
(1 Thessalonians 2:11-12)

> *Passing on the Father's love*
> **Leave an encouraging note for your child
> on the refrigerator or in a lunch box.**

☐ 53 _____

When a period of feasting had run its course, Job
would send and have them purified. Early in the
morning he would sacrifice a burnt offering for
each of them, thinking, "Perhaps my children have
sinned and cursed God in their hearts." This was
Job's regular custom. (Job 1:5)

> *Passing on the Father's love*
> **Pray with your wife tonight for each of
> your children, by name.**

□ 54 _____

Blessed is the man who does not walk in the counsel of the wicked. . . . But his delight is in the law of the Lord, and on his law he meditates day and night. He is like a tree planted by streams of water, which yields its fruit in season. (Psalm 1:1-3)

Passing on the Father's love
Plant a tree with your child, and watch it grow over the years.

□ 55 _____

Houses and wealth are inherited from parents, but a prudent wife is from the Lord. (Proverbs 19:14)

Passing on the Father's love
Ask your wife to suggest one area in which your fathering could use improvement.

□ 56 _____

And I pray that you, being rooted and established in love, may have power, together with all the saints, to grasp how wide and long and high and deep is the love of Christ. (Ephesians 3:17-18)

Passing on the Father's love
Climb the highest hill (or building) in town with your kids today.

A STRONG FINISH: If we don't father our children, someone else will, whether it's the TV, the public school system, the federal government, gang leaders, or a boyfriend or girlfriend.

☐ 57 _____

Like cold water to a weary soul is good news from a distant land. (Proverbs 25:25)

Passing on the Father's love
Give your college-bound child some self-addressed stamped envelopes to encourage her to write home. Be sure to write her back.

☐ 58 _____

I will instruct you (says the Lord) and guide you along the best pathway for your life; I will advise you and watch your progress. (Psalm 32:8, TLB)

Passing on the Father's love
Be a chaperon on your child's school field trip.

☐ 59 _____

No discipline seems pleasant at the time, but painful. Later on, however, it produces a harvest of righteousness and peace for those who have been trained by it. (Hebrews 12:11)

Passing on the Father's love
Tell your child an incident when you were disciplined as a child and what positive things you learned from it.

☐ 60 _____

In abundance of counselors there is victory. (Proverbs 24:6, NASB)

Passing on the Father's love
Go to the local bookstore, and check out their selection of books on fathering or parenting.

☐ 61 _____

I have set my rainbow in the clouds, and it will be the sign of the covenant between me and the earth. Whenever I bring clouds over the earth and the rainbow appears in the clouds, I will remember my covenant between me and you and all living creatures of every kind. (Genesis 9:13-15)

Passing on the Father's love
After the next rainstorm, go splash in the puddles with your kids, and rescue worms from the sidewalk.

☐ 62 _____

And the things you have heard me say in the presence of many witnesses entrust to reliable men who will also be qualified to teach others. (2 Timothy 2:2)

Passing on the Father's love
Let your child visit you at your workplace.

☐ 63 _____

The Lord disciplines those he loves, as a father the son he delights in. (Proverbs 3:12)

Passing on the Father's love
For instruction on effectively disciplining your children, read the updated classic, *The New Dare to Discipline,* by James Dobson (Tyndale).

A STRONG FINISH: Heredity does not equip a child with proper attitudes; children learn what they are taught. Dr. Luther Woodward

☐ 64 _____

And what more shall I say? I do not have time to tell about Gideon, Barak, Samson, Jephthah, David, Samuel and the prophets, who through faith conquered kingdoms, administered justice, and gained what was promised; who shut the mouths of lions, quenched the fury of the flames, and escaped the edge of the sword; whose weakness was turned to strength; and who became powerful in battle and routed foreign armies. . . . These were all commended for their faith. (Hebrews 11:32-34, 39)

Ask your child who is his all-time hero or heroine, and why.

☐ 65 _____

God said, "Let us make a man—someone like ourselves, to be the master of all life upon the earth and in the skies and in the seas." So God made man like his Maker. . . . Then God looked over all that he had made, and it was excellent in every way. (Genesis 1:26-27, 31, TLB)

Passing on the Father's love
Are you laying concrete anytime soon? Let your kids put their handprints in the wet cement. Scratch their names and the date.

☐ 66 _____

Can a mother forget the baby at her breast and have no compassion on the child she has borne? Though she may forget, I will not forget you! See, I have engraved you on the palms of my hands. (Isaiah 49:15-16)

Passing on the Father's love
Tell your daughters about the respect you have for motherhood.

☐ 67 _____

Listen, my son, to your father's instruction and do not forsake your mother's teaching. They will be a garland to grace your head and a chain to adorn your neck. (Proverbs 1:8-9)

Passing on the Father's love
Tell your kids something important that your mother taught you.

☐ 68 _____

He who works his land will have abundant food, but the one who chases fantasies will have his fill of poverty. (Proverbs 28:19)

Passing on the Father's love
Buy or make your child a piggy bank. Help him or her learn the value of saving money for a specific purpose. Check out a book such as *Raising Money-Smart Kids* by Ron and Judy Blue (Nelson).

☐ 69 _____

Honor your father and your mother, as the Lord your God has commanded you, so that you may live long and that it may go well with you in the land the Lord your God is giving you. (Deuteronomy 5:16)

Passing on the Father's love
Be Mom's servant with your kids for the day.

☐ 70 _____

Husbands, love your wives, just as Christ loved the church and gave himself up for her to make her holy, cleansing her by the washing with water through the word, and to present her to himself as a radiant church, without stain or wrinkle or any other blemish, but holy and blameless. (Ephesians 5:25-27)

Passing on the Father's love

Have a surprise "Who's the Best Mother in the World?" awards dinner with your children for their mother. Organize it like the Academy Awards, and have a number of categories where Mom wins every time.

A STRONG FINISH: When a father teaches his child a new lesson or a new skill, the child gets not only the benefit of the newly acquired skill but also the benefit of knowing that his father is concerned about his future and interested in his development. The child gets the skill and the emotional strength to use it.

Twelve Fathering Factors

1. Modeling. A committed father models behavior he wants his children to follow.

2. Dealing with Difficulties. A committed father provides leadership when faced with a problem, and the children are thus prepared to face similar challenges.

3. Committing Time to Children. A committed father takes time to be with his children.

4. Being a Financial Provider. A committed father accepts and fulfills his role of providing for the material needs of his children.

5. Showing Affection. A committed father communicates his affection to his children both verbally and nonverbally.

6. Allowing Freedom of Expression. A committed father encourages open communication of his children's thoughts, feelings, and actions. He responds without overreacting and with a sense of humor.

7. Spiritual Development. A committed father encourages his children to grow and develop spiritually by praying with them, by reading the Scriptures with them, and by actively leading them in participation in a local church or parish.

8. Knowing His Child. A committed father knows the unique characteristics of his child and the issues, activities, and people of his child's world.

9. Involvement in Education. A committed father is actively involved in providing his children with the necessary tools for living.

10. Involvement in Discipline. A committed father sets clear standards and limits for his children's behavior. He is able to discern when to discipline his children and knows appropriate and effective ways for doing so.

11. Marital Interaction. A committed father has a good relationship with his wife. He is aware of her needs and is dedicated to a stronger marriage, which provides security for his children.

12. Parental Discussion of Children.
A committed father openly discusses his children's development with his wife. He offers support to his wife and is receptive to the support she offers.

☐ 71 _____

Therefore the Lord blessed the Sabbath day and made it holy. (Exodus 20:11)

Passing on the Father's love
After church today, ask your kids what part of the service they think God enjoyed the most.

☐ 72 _____

Commit to the Lord whatever you do, and your plans will succeed. (Proverbs 16:3)

Passing on the Father's love

When planning a vacation, have the children calculate the cost and mileage for the trip.

☐ 73 _____

We have all had human fathers who disciplined us and we respected them for it. How much more should we submit to the Father of our spirits and live! (Hebrews 12:9)

Passing on the Father's love

Discuss one of your children's friends who needed discipline but had no one to provide it.

☐ 74 _____

Then [Jacob] gave them these instructions: . . . When Jacob had finished giving instructions to his sons, he drew his feet up into the bed, breathed his last and was gathered to his people. (Genesis 49:29, 33)

Passing on the Father's love

If you were on your deathbed, what is the one thing you would want to tell each of your children? Tell them today instead.

☐ 75 _____

Dear brothers, I am not writing out a new rule for you to obey, for it is an old one you have always had, right from the start. You have heard it all before. Yet it is always new, and works for you just as it did for Christ; and as we obey this commandment, *to love one another,* the darkness in our lives disappears and the new light of life in Christ shines in. (1 John 2:7-8, TLB)

Passing on the Father's love

Share a problem or struggle you are going through (if appropriate), and ask your child to pray for you.

☐ 76 _____

But ask the animals, and they will teach you, or the birds of the air, and they will tell you; or speak to the earth, and it will teach you, or let the fish of the sea inform you. Which of all these does not know that the hand of the Lord has done this? In his hand is the life of every creature and the breath of all mankind. (Job 12:7-10)

Passing on the Father's love

Make sure your kids are participating in the care of family pets.

☐ 77 _____

I kneel before the Father, from whom his whole family in heaven and on earth derives its name. I pray that out of his glorious riches he may strengthen you with power through his Spirit in your inner being. . . . Do not call anyone on earth "father," for you have one Father, and he is in heaven. (Ephesians 3:14-16; Matthew 23:9)

Passing on the Father's love

Write a meaningful paragraph in your daughter's or son's Bible, and then sign it "your earthly father."

A STRONG FINISH: To this day I remember being out playing catch with my dad. We were throwing the ball back and forth. He caught it and said to me, "This is the first day I've really felt I could throw my hardest to you." That struck me as being a big moment in my life. George Bush

☐ 78 _____

"Honor your father and mother"—which is
the first commandment with a promise—
"that it may go well with you and that you
may enjoy long life on the earth."
(Ephesians 6:2)

Passing on the Father's love
**Honor your father or mother by commit-
ting yourself to meet a need that they
have.**

_____

Fathers, do not exasperate your children; instead, bring them up in the training and instruction of the Lord. (Ephesians 6:4)

Passing on the Father's love
Ask your wife to tell you whenever you push your children too hard or too far.

_____

Young man, it's wonderful to be young! Enjoy every minute of it! . . . But realize that you must account to God for everything you do. (Ecclesiastes 11:9, TLB)

Passing on the Father's love
Have each child write up a "dream list." Have them include all kinds of dreams— things they want, places they'd like to go, and ways in which they would like to use the gifts and talents God has given them.

_____

The righteous will flourish like a palm tree, they will grow like a cedar of Lebanon; planted in the house of the Lord, they will flourish in the courts of our God. They will still bear fruit in old age, they will stay fresh and green, proclaiming, "The Lord is upright; he is my Rock, and there is no wickedness in him." (Psalm 92:12-15)

Passing on the Father's love
**Have your kids interview their grandparents
on tape; have them ask questions about you.**

☐ 82 _____

But I will establish my covenant with you [Noah], and
you will enter the ark—you and your sons and your
wife and your sons' wives with you. (Genesis 6:18)

Passing on the Father's love
**Ask your wife what you do that makes
her and your children feel protected.**

☐ 83 _____

Every good and perfect gift is from above, coming
down from the Father of the heavenly lights, who
does not change like shifting shadows. (James 1:17)

Passing on the Father's love
**For a long trip in the car, put together a
surprise bag of goodies, games, books,
and tapes. Every fifty miles, let the kids
take an item out of the bag.**

☐ 84 _____

My son, if your heart is wise, then my heart will be
glad; my inmost being will rejoice when your lips
speak what is right. (Proverbs 23:15-16)

Passing on the Father's love
**Ask your child what he or she would do
with a thousand dollars.**

A STRONG FINISH: We learn to father by following models. If you had a bad fathering model while growing up, you can find a new one.

☐ 85 _____

Fear the Lord, you his saints, for those who fear him lack nothing. . . . Come, my children, listen to me; I will teach you the fear of the Lord. (Psalm 34:9, 11)

Passing on the Father's love
Play a worship tape at home as you prepare for church. On the way to the service, discuss one aspect of worship.

☐ 86 _____

"Choose for yourselves this day whom you will serve. . . . But as for me and my household, we will serve the Lord." . . . "Far be it from us to forsake the Lord to serve other gods!" (Joshua 24:15-16)

Passing on the Father's love
Choose a verse from the Bible to use as your family motto.

☐ 87 _____

He remembers his covenant forever, the word he commanded, for a thousand generations, the covenant he made with Abraham, the oath he swore to Isaac. (Psalm 105:8)

Passing on the Father's love
Tell your children a story about your father and your grandfather.

☐ 88 _____

By faith Moses, when he was born, was hidden for three months by his parents, because they saw he was a beautiful child; and they were not afraid of the king's edict. (Hebrews 11:23, NASB)

Passing on the Father's love
Sometimes our culture exploits children, as in certain television shows and movies. Decide with your wife three ways in which you will protect your children.

_____

When he came to his senses, he said, ". . . I will set
out and go back to my father and say to him:
Father, I have sinned against heaven and against
you." So he got up and went to his father. (Luke
15:17-18, 20)

Passing on the Father's love
**Tell your children that, no matter what
they do, you are still their father and you
love them.**

_____

A generous man will prosper; he who refreshes
others will himself be refreshed. (Proverbs 11:25)

Passing on the Father's love
Take food to a needy family.

_____

"I will feed My flock and I will lead them to rest,"
declares the Lord God. "I will seek the lost, bring
back the scattered, bind up the broken, and
strengthen the sick." (Ezekiel 34:15-16, NASB)

Passing on the Father's love
**Ask your teenager what causes him the
greatest stress.**

**A STRONG FINISH: They never read your
resume at your funeral, and no one has died saying they wish they'd spent more time at the office.**

☐ 92 _____

Correct, rebuke and encourage—with great
patience and careful instruction. (2 Timothy 4:2)

Passing on the Father's love
**Put an encouraging note in the textbook
of your child's worst subject.**

☐ 93 _____

Look, he is coming with the clouds, and every eye
will see him. (Revelation 1:7)

Passing on the Father's love

On a cloudy afternoon, go outside with your kids, lie on your back in the grass, and point out pictures in the clouds.

☐ 94 _____

A patient man has great understanding, but a quick-tempered man displays folly. (Proverbs 14:29)

Passing on the Father's love

Ask your children, separately, to share one thing that "bugs" them about their brothers or sisters. Help them figure out how to deal with it.

☐ 95 _____

It has given me great joy to find some of your children walking in the truth, just as the Father commanded us. (2 John 1:4)

Passing on the Father's love

Next time your child makes you proud, "beam" outwardly, even if you're in public and you feel ridiculous doing it.

☐ 96 _____

Like newborn babes, long for the pure milk of the word, that by it you may grow in respect to salvation, if you have tasted the kindness of the Lord. (1 Peter 2:2-3, NASB)

Passing on the Father's love
Act out a Bible story as a family tonight.

☐ 97 _____

Fathers, do not embitter your children, or they will become discouraged. (Colossians 3:21)

Passing on the Father's love
Allow your child to express any negative feelings he has toward you, but in an appropriate manner.

☐ 98 _____

After three days they found [Jesus] in the temple courts, sitting among the teachers, listening to them and asking them questions. Everyone who heard him was amazed at his understanding and his answers. (Luke 2:46-47)

Passing on the Father's love
Listen to your child read *you* a story.

A STRONG FINISH: The simple fact that you own a Bible is communicating something valuable to your kids. Of course, owning a Bible but not reading it also communicates something powerful.

☐ 99 _____

All these are the twelve tribes of Israel, and this is
what their father [Jacob] said to them when he
blessed them, giving each the blessing appropriate
to him. (Genesis 49:28)

> *Passing on the Father's love*
> **Make a "toast" to one of the children at din-
> ner tonight. Do a different child each night.**

☐ 100 _____

And the boy Samuel continued to grow in stature
and in favor with the Lord and with men.
(1 Samuel 2:26)

> *Passing on the Father's love*
> **Measure the height of each of your children.**

☐ 101 _____

Do not forsake your friend and the friend of your
father. (Proverbs 27:10)

Passing on the Father's love

**Challenge each of your children to make
a new acquaintance or start a new friendship today. Tell them you will do the
same, and then compare notes tonight.**

☐ 102 _____

At that time Jesus said, "I praise you, Father, Lord
of heaven and earth, because you have hidden these
things from the wise and learned, and revealed
them to little children. Yes, Father, for this was
your good pleasure." (Matthew 11:25-26)

Passing on the Father's love

**Ask your son or daughter to describe the
most difficult problem our nation is facing.**

☐ 103 _____

My dear brothers, take note of this: Everyone should
be quick to listen, slow to speak and slow to become
angry, for man's anger does not bring about the righteous life that God desires. (James 1:19-20)

Passing on the Father's love

**Talk to your kids about how you react
when you are angry; then describe how
you would prefer to react.**

All your sons will be taught by the Lord, and great will be your children's peace. (Isaiah 54:13)

Passing on the Father's love

Have an honest talk about sex. Tell your son or daughter the Lord's plan and the consequences of premarital sex.

☐ 105 _____

Therefore go and make disciples of all nations, baptizing them in the name of the Father and of the Son and of the Holy Spirit, and teaching them to obey everything I have commanded you. (Matthew 28:19-20)

Passing on the Father's love

Pray for one of your neighbors who doesn't know Christ. Share the gospel with that person, and tell your kids about how the person responded.

A STRONG FINISH: I truly believe that the lot of those that suffer is more enviable than the people who seem to be set apart, untouched, like a piece of fine china in a locked cabinet. Without dark clouds in our lives we would never know the joy of sunshine. Billy Graham

WEEK 16

☐ 106 _____

But while he was still a long way off, his father saw
him and was filled with compassion for him; he ran
to his son, threw his arms around him and kissed
him. (Luke 15:20)

Passing on the Father's love
**Tell your kids "I love you," even if you've
said it already this month.**

☐ 107 _____

Tell it to your children, and let your children tell it
to their children, and their children to the next
generation. (Joel 1:3)

Tell your children the gospel; as God allows, be the one to lead your children to faith in Christ Jesus.

☐ 108 _____

I know what it is to be in need, and I know what it is to have plenty. I have learned the secret of being content in any and every situation, whether well fed or hungry, whether living in plenty or in want. (Philippians 4:12)

Passing on the Father's love
Tell your children about a time when you were "in want" and how you handled it.

☐ 109 _____

Then he threw his arms around his brother Benjamin and wept, and Benjamin embraced him, weeping. And he kissed all his brothers and wept over them. (Genesis 45:14-15)

Passing on the Father's love
Discuss your children's feelings and thoughts about each other. Help them appreciate the characteristics of their siblings.

☐ 110 _____

Give to Caesar what is Caesar's, and to God what is God's. (Matthew 22:21)

Passing on the Father's love
Tell your kids how much they saved you as tax deductions this year!

☐ 111 _____

From the lips of children and infants you have ordained praise because of your enemies, to silence the foe and the avenger. (Psalm 8:2)

Passing on the Father's love
Let your children plan and lead a family worship time.

☐ 112 _____

Endure hardship with us like a good soldier of Christ Jesus. (2 Timothy 2:3)

Passing on the Father's love
Visit a local military base or National Guard armory.

A STRONG FINISH: Fathers make *unique* and *irreplaceable* contributions to the lives of their children. Dr. Wade Horn

☐ 113 _____

But now the Lord who created you . . . says, ". . . I
have called you by name; you are mine." (Isaiah
43:1, TLB)

Passing on the Father's love
**Be sure to introduce your children by
name whenever you are together in the
presence of other adults.**

☐ 114 _____

I will be careful to lead a blameless life—when
will you come to me? I will walk in my house with

blameless heart. I will set before my eyes no vile thing. (Psalm 101:2-3)

Passing on the Father's love
Be a spiritual safety inspector: Ask yourself if there is anything in the house that is morally dangerous to you and your family.

☐ 115 _____

Ask the former generations and find out what their fathers learned. (Job 8:8)

Passing on the Father's love
Have your dad tell your children a story about his father.

☐ 116 _____

Therefore, since we are surrounded by such a great cloud of witnesses, let us throw off everything that hinders and the sin that so easily entangles, and let us run with perseverance the race marked out for us. (Hebrews 12:1)

Passing on the Father's love
Build a makeshift obstacle course in your backyard. Time the kids as they race through it.

☐ 117 _____

Trust in the Lord and do good; dwell in the land and enjoy safe pasture. (Psalm 37:3)

Passing on the Father's love
Take the whole family on an evening walk through the neighborhood. Feel free to stop and chat with people you see.

☐ 118 _____

Let us not become weary in doing good, for at the proper time we will reap a harvest if we do not give up. (Galatians 6:9)

Passing on the Father's love
Help your kids plant their own small garden.

☐ 119 _____

I have no greater joy than to hear that my children are walking in the truth. (3 John 1:4)

Passing on the Father's love
Tell your daughter about a girl you know who got pregnant outside of marriage. Describe how this pregnancy affected her life.

A STRONG FINISH: Children are remarkable for their intelligence and ardor, for their curiosity, their intolerance of shams, the clarity and truthfulness of their vision. Aldous Huxley

☐ 120 _____

Similarly, encourage the young men to be self-controlled. In everything set them an example by doing what is good. (Titus 2:6-7)

Passing on the Father's love
Help your children do their chores.

☐ 121 _____

Dear children, let us not love with words or tongue but with actions and in truth. (1 John 3:18)

Passing on the Father's love

Think of five ways you demonstrate your love for your children. Then each time you do those tasks be sure to communicate your love through words and actions.

☐ 122 _____

And whatever you do, whether in word or deed, do it all in the name of the Lord Jesus, giving thanks to God the Father through him. (Colossians 3:17)

Passing on the Father's love

Have everyone write a letter of thanks to God. (Have the young ones dictate their letter to you.) Then have everyone read them around the dinner table.

☐ 123 _____

Joseph named his firstborn Manasseh and said, "It is because God has made me forget all my trouble and all my father's household." (Genesis 41:51)

Passing on the Father's love

Explain to your child the meaning of his name (or your reasons for naming him as you did).

☐ 124 _____

For this reason a man will leave his father and mother and be united to his wife, and they will become one flesh. (Genesis 2:24)

Passing on the Father's love
Ask your wife if there are any ways she feels you are unfairly comparing her to your mother.

☐ 125 _____

Make it your ambition to lead a quiet life, to mind your own business and to work . . . just as we told you, so that your daily life may win the respect of outsiders. (1 Thessalonians 4:11-12)

Passing on the Father's love
Do a practice job interview with your child. Guide her through the process; then hire her.

☐ 126 _____

"In your anger do not sin": Do not let the sun go down while you are still angry. (Ephesians 4:26)

Passing on the Father's love
Teach your child which expressions of anger are not appropriate; then talk about some appropriate ways to vent anger (e.g., talking to someone, exercise, etc.).

A STRONG FINISH: The faithful father does his duty prayerfully and trusts God for those things he cannot control.

WEEK **19**

☐ 127 _____

As he looked about and saw his brother Benjamin, his own mother's son, he asked, "Is this your youngest brother, the one you told me about?" And he said "God be gracious to you, my son." (Genesis 43:29)

Passing on the Father's love
Have a family portrait taken.

☐ 128 _____

Be completely humble and gentle; be patient, bearing with one another in love. (Ephesians 4:2)

Passing on the Father's love
Take time to unwind before leaving for home after work. You'll be more responsive to your kids when you're not trying to relax at the same time.

☐ 129 _____

Their children, who do not know this law, must hear it and learn to fear the Lord your God as long as you live in the land you are crossing the Jordan to possess. (Deuteronomy 31:13)

Passing on the Father's love
Share with your kids something you did as a child that you regret. Point out what you learned as a result.

☐ 130 _____

By faith Noah, when warned about things not yet seen, in holy fear built an ark to save his family. (Hebrews 11:7)

Passing on the Father's love
Discuss with your wife what you consider to be the greatest threats against your family, and then pray together against them.

☐ 131 _____

It is God's will that you should be sanctified: that you should avoid sexual immorality; that each of you should learn to control his own body in a way that is holy and honorable. (1 Thessalonians 4:3-4)

Passing on the Father's love
By the way you wrestle and rough-house with your children, you demonstrate self-control and what is acceptable.

☐ 132 _____

I urge, then, first of all, that requests, prayers, intercession and thanksgiving be made for everyone—for kings and all those in authority, that we may live peaceful and quiet lives in all godliness and holiness. (1 Timothy 2:1-2)

Passing on the Father's love
Conduct a "prayer search" through the New Testament, assigning each family member his or her own book or chapter to search in.

☐ 133 _____

Beloved, do not imitate what is evil, but what is good. (3 John 1:11, NASB)

Passing on the Father's love
Take your kids to an art museum; pose like the sculptures and take pictures.

A STRONG FINISH: A real tradition ... appears as an heirloom, a heritage one receives on condition of making it bear fruit before passing it on to one's descendants. Igor Stravinsky

☐ 134 _____

Fix these words of mine in your hearts and
minds. . . . Teach them to your children, talking
about them when you sit at home and when you
walk along the road, when you lie down and when
you get up. (Deuteronomy 11:18-19)

Passing on the Father's love
**After church today, ask your kids, "What
did you learn from the lesson?"**

☐ 135 _____

For God did not give us a spirit of timidity, but a
spirit of power, of love and of self-discipline.
(2 Timothy 1:7)

Tell your children who your three favorite heroes are. Describe qualities in them that you are seeking to model.

☐ 136 _____

Do not oppress the widow or the fatherless, the alien or the poor. In your hearts do not think evil of each other. (Zechariah 7:10)

Passing on the Father's love
Talk about a friend of your children who is fatherless. Ask your kids how he or she is doing, and invite this person on an outing with your family.

☐ 137 _____

Carry each other's burdens, and in this way you will fulfill the law of Christ. (Galatians 6:2)

Passing on the Father's love
Read the parable of the Good Samaritan with your kids; then ask them who at school needs their friendship and mercy.

☐ 138 _____

Husbands ought to love their wives as their own bodies. He who loves his wife loves himself. (Ephesians 5:28)

Passing on the Father's love
Be polite to your wife; compliment her in your children's presence.

☐ 139 _____

One [of Moses' sons] was named Gershom, for Moses said, "I have become an alien in a foreign land"; and the other was named Eliezer, for he said, "My father's God was my helper; he saved me from the sword of Pharaoh." (Exodus 18:3-4)

Passing on the Father's love
Advise your kids on what to do in the event of a natural disaster (tornado, earthquake, etc.).

☐ 140 _____

In all your ways acknowledge Him, and He will make your paths straight. (Proverbs 3:6, NASB)

Passing on the Father's love
On your vacation, tell your kids the destination, give them a map, and let them figure out the roads to take.

A STRONG FINISH: Your children are more than just "the kids." Each one is a unique human being. However much we think in terms of "the family," we must also be careful to recognize each member of the group as an individual.

Lighten Up!

➤ Give your child a big hug and a kiss on the cheek. Then say, "I needed that!"

➤ Get out the sprinkler and have a water fight with the kids. Go buy squirt guns or make two dozen water balloons; then declare war on your kids. Make sure they win!

➤ Carry your young children on your shoulders, and parade around the house.

➤ Take your kids to a professional or college sports game.

➤ Go blueberry or strawberry picking.

➤ On a weekend morning, climb into bed with your young child.

➤ Lie on the lawn with your children at night, and stare at the stars.

➤ Go up to your child and say, "That's what I like about you, you're [fill in the blank]."

➢ Drive to the nearest candy store with your child, and stare in the window. Treat yourself and your child.

➢ Have the car washed at a drive-through car wash, with you and your kids all inside the car.

➢ Go rake some leaves with your child; then fall in and bury yourself.

➢ Tickle your son or daughter (but don't let it get torturous).

➢ Plan an overnight camp-out in the back-yard or at a nearby campground.

➢ Wash the family pet with your kids.

➢ Go sledding with your child. Double up and yell as you go down the hill. If there's no snow around, try a wagon.

➢ Let the kids pick out your clothes for the day.

➢ Go out with your kids this evening, and capture lightning bugs.

➢ Go to a lake or stream with your kids, and skip stones.

➢ Arrange to meet your kids in the park today for a picnic lunch.

- Make up a "round-robin" story, where everyone takes turns contributing one sentence at a time.

- Take a flashlight and help your kids hunt night crawlers in your backyard.

- Attend your daughter's tea party.

- Tonight at dinner, switch roles with your kids. Pretend you're the kids and they're the parents.

- Let your kids play dress-up with your clothes and have a fashion show.

- Play a game by declaring one hour of silence. Turn off the TV and stereo and unplug the phone. Allow only sign language communication.

- Help your children make dinner for your wife.

- Publish a family newsletter, and let your kids contribute articles and drawings.

☐ 141 _____

By day the Lord directs his love, at night his song is with me—a prayer to the God of my life. (Psalm 42:8)

Passing on the Father's love
**Go for a walk after dark with your child.
Listen closely to the night sounds.**

☐ 142 _____

[The kingdom of heaven] will be like a man going on a journey, who called his servants and entrusted his property to them. To one he gave five talents of money, to another two talents, and to another one talent, each according to his ability. (Matthew 25:14-15)

Passing on the Father's love

Loan your child five dollars to invest in something that will make more money. Arrange for him to repay you after a month; let him keep the profits.

☐ 143 _____

Two are better than one, because they have a good return for their work: If one falls down, his friend can help him up. . . . Though one may be overpowered, two can defend themselves. A cord of three strands is not quickly broken. (Ecclesiastes 4:9-10, 12)

Passing on the Father's love

Remind your children that your whole family is on the same team. Describe how a team works together to win a game.

☐ 144 _____

But you know of his proven worth that he served with me in the furtherance of the gospel like a child serving his father. (Philippians 2:22, NASB)

Passing on the Father's love

Engage in a special work project with your child, whether it's home remodeling, making a gift, or fixing a bike or car. Take the extra time to involve them.

Do not neglect to show hospitality to strangers, for by doing that some have entertained angels without knowing it. (Hebrews 13:2)

Passing on the Father's love
Plan a barbecue where you are the cook.

Then our sons in their youth will be like well-nurtured plants, and our daughters will be like pillars carved to adorn a palace. (Psalm 144:12)

Passing on the Father's love
Spend some time going through the family scrapbook or photo album with your children, talking about major events and changes in their lives.

It is better not to vow than to make a vow and not fulfill it. (Ecclesiastes 5:5)

Passing on the Father's love
Make a promise to your children today. Let it be one that you can deliver on.

A STRONG FINISH: Every man who comes into her life will be measured, for better or worse, against me. . . . If a man has cherished his daughter, she will probably choose men who will cherish her. Richard Wesley

☐ 148 _____

Do not withhold good from those who deserve it, when it is in your power to act. (Proverbs 3:27)

Passing on the Father's love
Practice some sport or activity with your child. Tell her how she is improving.

☐ 149 _____

You know your father and his men; they are fighters, and as fierce as a wild bear robbed of her cubs. Besides, your father is an experienced fighter; . . . all Israel knows that your father is a fighter and that those with him are brave. (2 Samuel 17:8, 10)

Passing on the Father's love
Tell your children a story about a time when you had to defend your family in some manner.

☐ 150 _____

Each of you must respect his mother and father. (Leviticus 19:3)

Passing on the Father's love
Tell your children what you remember most about your parents.

☐ 151 _____

[Jesus] appointed twelve—designating them apostles—that they might be with him and that he might send them out to preach and to have authority to drive out demons. These are the twelve: . . . James son of Zebedee and his brother John (to them he gave the name Boanerges, which means Sons of Thunder). (Mark 3:14-17)

Passing on the Father's love
Think of an affectionate nickname for your child—and make sure he or she approves.

☐ 152 _____

They will be my people, and I will be their God. I will give them singleness of heart and action, so that they will always fear me for their own good and the good of their children after them. I will make an everlasting covenant with them: I will never stop doing good to them, and I will inspire them to fear me, so that they will never turn away from me. I will rejoice in doing them good and will assuredly plant them in this land with all my heart and soul. (Jeremiah 32:38-41)

Passing on the Father's love
Show your kids your wedding album, and talk about what a marriage covenant means.

☐ 153 _____

Daughters of Jerusalem, I charge you by the gazelle and by the does of the field: Do not arouse or awaken love until it so desires. (Song of Songs 2:7)

Passing on the Father's love
Discuss with your wife what age you think is appropriate for your kids to start dating, and then talk with them about it.

☐ 154 _____

He will take pity on the weak and the needy and save the needy from death. He will rescue them from oppression and violence, for precious is their blood in his sight. (Psalm 72:13-14)

Passing on the Father's love

Volunteer to work in the church nursery
with your son or daughter.

A STRONG FINISH: If we model grace under
pressure during a crisis and take positive action,
we not only help our children survive the immedi-
ate crisis but also help them prepare for future
ones.

WEEK **23**

☐ 155 _____

Do not be misled: "Bad company corrupts good character." (1 Corinthians 15:33)

Passing on the Father's love
The next time your child's friends are over at your house, spend some time talking to them and getting to know them.

☐ 156 _____

Treat younger men as brothers, older women as

mothers, and younger women as sisters, with absolute purity. (1 Timothy 5:1-2)

Passing on the Father's love

Teach your children how to recognize sexually inappropriate and abusive behavior. Tell them how to resist this behavior, and urge them to notify you immediately if anyone attempts such action toward them.

☐ 157 _____

The righteous man leads a blameless life; blessed are his children after him. (Proverbs 20:7)

Passing on the Father's love

Tell your children something positive you learned from your father.

☐ 158 _____

Come to me and I will give you rest—all of you who work so hard beneath a heavy yoke. Wear my yoke—for it fits perfectly—and let me teach you; for I am gentle and humble, and you shall find rest for your souls; for I give you only light burdens. (Matthew 11:28-30, TLB)

Passing on the Father's love

Tell your child about a struggle you've been having. Let him minister to you.

We taught the Scriptures to some women who came. One of them was Lydia, a saleswoman from Thyatira, a merchant of purple cloth. She was already a worshiper of God and as she listened to us, the Lord opened her heart and she accepted all that Paul was saying. She was baptized along with all her household and asked us to be her guests. (Acts 16:13-15, TLB)

Passing on the Father's love
Ask your child what she wants to be when she grows up, and then take her to visit such a workplace.

The word of the Lord came to me: "Son of man, set forth an allegory and tell the house of Israel a parable. Say to them, 'This is what the Sovereign Lord says: A great eagle with powerful wings, long feathers and full plumage of varied colors came to Lebanon. . . .'" (Ezekiel 17:1-3)

Passing on the Father's love
Choose a book to read to your children from which you can read one chapter each night (for example, *The Island of the Blue Dolphins*).

The world and its desires pass away, but the man who does the will of God lives forever. (1 John 2:17)

Passing on the Father's love

Make plans to join thousands of other Christian men at a Promise Keepers conference during one weekend. Consider taking your son.

A STRONG FINISH: Dad, if you're not around, your wife and children will learn to live without you. Greg Johnson and Mike Yorkey

☐ 162 _____

A wise son heeds his father's instruction, but a mocker does not listen to rebuke. (Proverbs 13:1)

Passing on the Father's love
Teach your kids about prescription drugs—their use and abuse.

☐ 163 _____

Finally, brothers, good-by. Aim for perfection, listen to my appeal, be of one mind, live in peace. And the God of love and peace will be with you.

Greet one another with a holy kiss. All the saints send their greetings. May the grace of the Lord Jesus Christ, and the love of God, and the fellowship of the Holy Spirit be with you all. (2 Corinthians 13:11-14)

Passing on the Father's love
Encourage your wife by praising something you like in her family, your in-laws.

□ 164 _____

For this is what the Lord says: "I will extend peace to her like a river, and the wealth of nations like a flooding stream; you will nurse and be carried on her arm and dandled on her knees." (Isaiah 66:12)

Passing on the Father's love
Spend a quiet time in your child's bedroom with him before he falls asleep.

□ 165 _____

The Lord your God is with you, he is mighty to save. He will take great delight in you, he will quiet you with his love, he will rejoice over you with singing. (Zephaniah 3:17)

Passing on the Father's love
Prepare dinner and feed your infant or small child.

☐ 166

Nowhere in all the land were there found women as beautiful as Job's daughters, and their father granted them an inheritance along with their brothers. (Job 42:15)

Passing on the Father's love
Point out to your adolescent daughter signs you see of her growing into a woman.

☐ 167

So Daniel was rushed in to see the king. The king asked him, "Are you the Daniel brought from Israel as a captive by King Nebuchadnezzar? I have heard that you have the spirit of the gods within you and that you are filled with enlightenment and wisdom." (Daniel 5:13-14, TLB)

Passing on the Father's love
Describe a man or woman of outstanding character to your children.

☐ 168

Come out, you daughters of Zion, and look at King Solomon wearing the crown, the crown with which his mother crowned him on the day of his wedding, the day his heart rejoiced. Song of Songs 3:11

Passing on the Father's love
Take your wife on a double date with your teenager.

A STRONG FINISH: Clearly, children without an involved father are vulnerable to the withering winds of a society in rebellion against God. The psalmist cursed the evil household with fatherlessness (Ps. 109:9) because, in the ancient Near East, the father provided protection from the world.

☐ 169 _____

I will rejoice over Jerusalem and take delight in my people; the sound of weeping and of crying will be heard in it no more. Never again will there be in it an infant who lives but a few days, or an old man who does not live out his years. (Isaiah 65:19-20)

Passing on the Father's love
Watch your child while he sleeps.

☐ 170 _____

An intelligent mind acquires knowledge, and the ear of the wise seeks knowledge. (Proverbs 18:15, NRSV)

Passing on the Father's love
Tell your children about a book you are reading.

☐ 171 _____

He heals the brokenhearted and binds up their wounds. (Psalm 147:3)

Passing on the Father's love
As your schedule allows, stay home with your child one day when he is sick. Be his personal attendant that day.

☐ 172 _____

Children's children are a crown to the aged, and parents are the pride of their children. (Proverbs 17:6)

Passing on the Father's love
Let your child use you as his "show-and-tell" at school.

☐ 173 _____

For whatever things were written before were written for our learning, that we through the patience and comfort of the Scriptures might have hope. (Romans 15:4, NKJV)

Passing on the Father's love
Read a paragraph, chapter, or book to your children that you feel is vital to their growth. Discuss their reactions to it.

You are to live clean, innocent lives as children of God in a dark world full of people who are crooked and stubborn. Shine out among them like beacon lights. (Philippians 2:15, TLB)

Passing on the Father's love
When you are with the kids, stop the car and pick up some trash along the road.

Therefore comfort each other and edify one another, just as you also are doing. (1 Thessalonians 5:11, NKJV)

Passing on the Father's love
Ask your wife what one thing you do that is most supportive of her mothering.

A STRONG FINISH: Dr. Ross Campbell, a psychiatrist who specializes in working with children, has discovered that in all his reading and experience, he has never known of one sexually disoriented person who had a warm, loving, and affectionate father. Gary Smalley

☐ 176 _____

A man finds joy in giving an apt reply—
and how good is a timely word! (Proverbs
15:23)

Passing on the Father's love
**Buy five or ten postcards for each child,
and on each one write how much you
love him or her and one hope you have
for his/her life. Mail them all over the
next month or so.**

☐ 177 _____

All hard work brings a profit, but mere talk leads only to poverty. (Proverbs 14:23)

Passing on the Father's love
Do a household chore with your kids: sweep the floor, dust the shelves, or clean the cupboards.

☐ 178 _____

He has delivered us from such a deadly peril, and he will deliver us. On him we have set our hope that he will continue to deliver us. (2 Corinthians 1:10)

Passing on the Father's love
Advise your children about how to respond to strangers.

☐ 179 _____

Reckless words pierce like a sword, but the tongue of the wise brings healing. Truthful lips endure forever, but a lying tongue lasts only a moment. (Proverbs 12:18-19)

Passing on the Father's love
Inform your children what rules you and your wife have set regarding use of the telephone.

☐ 180 _____

Love is patient. (1 Corinthians 13:4)

Passing on the Father's love
Make a point to participate with your child in an activity he or she particularly likes.

☐ 181 _____

Make them pure and holy through teaching them your words of truth. (John 17:17, TLB)

Passing on the Father's love
Pray with each of your children alone— just the two of you—instead of always with the entire family or vice-versa, if your custom is the reverse.

☐ 182 _____

Do nothing out of selfish ambition or vain conceit, but in humility consider others better than your-selves. Each of you should look not only to your own interests, but also to the interests of others. (Philippians 2:3-4)

Passing on the Father's love
Recite the names of your kids' best friends; ask them to recite the names of yours.

A STRONG FINISH: An effective father sees the family as a divinely equipped team. He discovers what unique contributions each of his children can make to the family goals and utilizes them efficiently.

☐ 183 _____

Like arrows in the hands of a warrior are sons born
in one's youth. Blessed is the man whose quiver is
full of them. (Psalm 127:4-5)

Passing on the Father's love
**Plan a fishing expedition and bait your
child's hook.**

☐ 184 _____

Do not be anxious about anything, but in everything, by prayer and petition, with thanksgiving,

present your requests to God. And the peace of God, which transcends all understanding, will guard your hearts and your minds in Christ Jesus. (Philippians 4:6-7)

Passing on the Father's love
Pray with your kids at bedtime.

☐ 185 _____

Everyone who believes that Jesus is the Christ is born of God, and everyone who loves the father loves his child as well. (1 John 5:1)

Passing on the Father's love
Take a surprise "care package" to a single-parent home.

☐ 186 _____

Rescue me, O God! Lord, hurry to my aid! they are after my life and delight in hurting me. Confuse them! Shame them! Stop them! Don't let them keep on mocking me! But fill the followers of God with joy. Let those who love your salvation exclaim, "What a wonderful God he is!" But I am in deep trouble. Rush to my aid, for only you can help and save me. O Lord, don't delay. (Psalm 70, TLB)

Passing on the Father's love
Ask your child, "What is something that really upsets you?"

☐ 187 _____

Which of you fathers, if your son asks for a
fish will give him a snake instead? Or if he
asks for an egg, will give him a scorpion? If
you then, though you are evil, know how to
give good gifts to your children, how much
more will your Father in heaven give the
Holy Spirit to those who ask him! (Luke
11:13)

Passing on the Father's love
Teach your kids how to wrap a present.

☐ 188 _____

Whoever wants to become great among you must
be your servant, and whoever wants to be first
must be your slave—just as the Son of Man did not
come to be served, but to serve, and to give his life
as a ransom for many. (Matthew 20:26-27)

Passing on the Father's love
Take your child for a haircut.

☐ 189 _____

If you walk in my ways and obey my statutes and
commands as David your father did, I will give you
a long life. (1 Kings 3:14)

Passing on the Father's love
**Have your child (or each child) pick one
of the Ten Commandments. Talk together**

about how following that commandment could lead to a longer life.

A STRONG FINISH: The most important thing a father can do for his children is to love their mother. Father Hesburg

WEEK **28**

☐ 190 _____

He who walks with the wise grows wise, but a
companion of fools suffers harm. (Proverbs 13:20)

Passing on the Father's love
Encourage your adolescent to begin dating in groups first.

☐ 191 _____

From the rising of the sun to the place where it sets,
the name of the Lord is to be praised. (Psalm 113:3)

Passing on the Father's love
Go somewhere where you and your children can watch the sunset together.

☐ 192 _____

Teach a righteous man and he will add to his learning. (Proverbs 9:9)

Passing on the Father's love
Sign up for lessons (skiing, parachuting, pottery, etc.) with your child.

☐ 193 _____

Do your best to present yourself to God as one approved, a workman who does not need to be ashamed and who correctly handles the word of truth. (2 Timothy 2:15)

Passing on the Father's love
Get your child a hammer, nails, and some boards, and let him hammer away.

☐ 194 _____

Sons are a heritage from the Lord, children a reward from him. (Psalm 127:3)

Passing on the Father's love
Go on a family picnic.

☐ 195 _____

But I tell you that men will have to give account on the day of judgment for every careless word they have spoken. For by your words you will be acquitted, and by your words you will be condemned. (Matthew 12:36-37)

Passing on the Father's love
Ask each child if you have ever said anything careless that has hurt his or her feelings. If so, apologize.

☐ 196 _____

And whoever welcomes a little child like this in my name welcomes me. (Matthew 18:5)

Passing on the Father's love
Finger paint with your young children.

A STRONG FINISH: The only training which really matters is given within the home, and . . . there are no teachers so effective for good or evil as parents are. William Barclay

☐ 197 _____

See, I will send you the prophet Elijah before that great and dreadful day of the Lord comes. He will turn the hearts of the fathers to their children, and the hearts of the children to their fathers. (Malachi 4:5-6)

Passing on the Father's love
Tell your children your heartfelt dreams for each of them.

☐ 198 _____

You are enthroned as the Holy One; you are the praise of Israel. In you our fathers put their trust;

they trusted and you delivered them. They cried to you and were saved; in you they trusted and were not disappointed. (Psalm 22:3-5)

Passing on the Father's love
At the next family crisis, gather the whole family together for prayer to demonstrate your dependence on God.

☐ 199 _____

Is not wisdom found among the aged? Does not long life bring understanding? (Job 12:12)

Passing on the Father's love
Have your mother tell your children a story about her mother.

☐ 200 _____

If any of you lacks wisdom, he should ask God, who gives generously to all without finding fault, and it will be given to him. (James 1:5)

Passing on the Father's love
Take time to ask God for specific help in raising your children.

☐ 201 _____

Praise be to . . . the Father of compassion and the God of all comfort, who comforts us in all our troubles, so that we can comfort those in any trouble with the comfort we ourselves have received from God. (2 Corinthians 1:3-4)

Passing on the Father's love
Share with your child how you have struggled in an area that is difficult for him or her.

☐ 202 _____

As the Father has loved me, so have I loved you. (John 15:9)

Passing on the Father's love
Tell your kids "I love you," even if you have said so four times already this year.

☐ 203 _____

When you walk, they will guide you; when you sleep, they will watch over you; when you awake, they will speak to you. For these commands are a lamp, this teaching is a light, and the corrections of discipline are the way to life. (Proverbs 6:22-23)

Passing on the Father's love
Ask yourself what is the most important thing you need to discuss with your child in the next six months.

A STRONG FINISH: By all means see to it that families have access to good books. Richard Baxter

WEEK 30

☐ 204 _____

Yet he was merciful; he forgave their iniquities and did not destroy them. Time after time he restrained his anger and did not stir up his full wrath. He remembered that they were but flesh, a passing breeze that does not return. (Psalm 78:38-39)

Passing on the Father's love
Today, when you think of something about your child that is irritating or that

requires a lot of patience from you, think about what *you* were like at that age!

☐ 205 _____

You must not oppress a stranger in any way; remember, you yourselves were foreigners in the land of Egypt. (Exodus 22:21, TLB)

Passing on the Father's love
Teach your children some words of a foreign language.

☐ 206 _____

The father of a righteous man has great joy; he who has a wise son delights in him. (Proverbs 23:24)

Passing on the Father's love
Ask your child "How was your day?" or "How's your week going?"

☐ 207 _____

Rejoice that your names are written in heaven. (Luke 10:20)

Passing on the Father's love
Leading your family in a worship time at home is one of the most important things you can do as a father. Sing the Doxology and a few songs and have each member give thanks to the Lord for something specific.

☐ 208 _____

The trumpeters and singers joined in unison, as with one voice, to give praise and thanks to the Lord. Accompanied by trumpets, cymbals and other instruments, they raised their voices in praise to the Lord and sang: "He is good; his love endures forever." (2 Chronicles 5:13)

Passing on the Father's love
Make musical instruments and start a family band.

☐ 209 _____

His heart is secure, he will have no fear. (Psalm 112:8)

Passing on the Father's love
Take your child to school during the break between grades so that he or she can meet the new teacher.

☐ 210 _____

See, I have taught you decrees and laws as the Lord my God commanded me, so that you may follow them in the land you are entering to take possession of it. Observe them carefully, for this will show your wisdom and understanding to the nations, who will hear about all these decrees and say, "Surely this great nation is a wise and understanding people." What other nation is so great as to have their gods near them the way the

Lord our God is near us whenever we pray to him? And what other nation is so great as to have such righteous decrees and laws as this body of laws I am setting before you today?
(Deuteronomy 4:5-8)

Passing on the Father's love
Discuss with your wife appropriate limits for your children's television viewing. Then discuss them with your kids.

A STRONG FINISH: To discipline a child is not to punish him for stepping out of line, but to teach that child the way he ought to go. Discipline therefore includes everything that you do in order to help children learn. Henry R. Brandt

"I-CAN's" of Fathering

I — An **involved** father plays, works, tends to daily routines, attends activities, and just spends unstructured time with his children.

C — A **consistent** father is predictable. His children know what to expect from him.

A — An **aware** father has knowledge and understanding of his children and their world.

N— A **nurturant** father responds to the emotional needs of his children through verbal and physical affirmation.

☐ 211 _____

O Lord, you have searched me and you know me.
You know when I sit and when I rise; you perceive my thoughts from afar. . . . You are familiar
with all my ways. (Psalm 139:1-3)

Passing on the Father's love
**Ask your child what he likes to do in his
spare time.**

Her husband is respected at the city gate, where he takes his seat among the elders of the land. (Proverbs 31:23)

Passing on the Father's love

Ask your children to name the fathers of your community or church body. Then ask them why they chose those men.

By faith Jacob, when he was dying, blessed each of Joseph's sons, and worshiped as he leaned on the top of his staff. (Hebrews 11:21)

Passing on the Father's love

Point out a positive character trait about your child. Tell her how that trait is common to some famous person.

Hear my voice when I call, O Lord; be merciful to me and answer me. My heart says of you, "Seek his face!" Your face, Lord, I will seek. Do not hide your face from me, do not turn your servant away in anger; you have been my helper. Do not reject me or forsake me, O God my Savior. Though my father and mother forsake me, the Lord will receive me. (Psalm 27:7-10)

Passing on the Father's love

Talk about a foster child your children

know. Explain how God is being a father to him or her.

☐ 215 _____

All Scripture is God-breathed and is useful for teaching, rebuking, correcting and training in righteousness, so that the man of God may be thoroughly equipped for every good work. (2 Timothy 3:16-17)

Passing on the Father's love
Show your children the first Bible you had. Tell them what it meant to you then and what it means to you now.

☐ 216 _____

Pleasant words are a honeycomb, sweet to the soul and healing to the bones. (Proverbs 16:24)

Passing on the Father's love
Call your child while you are at work just to say hi.

☐ 217 _____

Jehovah is King! Let all the earth rejoice! Tell the farthest islands to be glad. . . . The heavens declare his perfect righteousness; every nation sees his glory. Let those who worship idols be disgraced—all who brag about their worthless gods—for every god must bow to him! (Psalm 97:1, 6-7, TLB)

Passing on the Father's love

Get your kids up early this Saturday, and take them for a walk to watch the sunrise.

A STRONG FINISH: God has built into each man the natural ability to be the very loving leader his family needs. Gary Smalley and John Trent

☐ 218 _____

Be strong and courageous, because you will lead these people to inherit the land I swore to their forefathers to give them. Be strong and very courageous. (Joshua 1:6-7)

Passing on the Father's love
Share positive things that have come to you and your family as a result of a problem you have faced.

☐ 219 _____

For he knows how we are formed, he remembers that we are dust. (Psalm 103:14)

Passing on the Father's love
Go get a physical. Make sure your children's father is in good shape.

☐ 220 _____

But the angel said to him: "Do not be afraid, Zechariah; your prayer has been heard. Your wife Elizabeth will bear you a son, and you are to give him the name John. He will be a joy and delight to you, and many will rejoice because of his birth. (Luke 1:13-14)

Passing on the Father's love
If you and your wife are expecting a baby, consider keeping a journal for your unborn child and then sharing it with your child when he or she is older.

☐ 221 _____

This day I call heaven and earth as witnesses against you that I have set before you life and death, blessings and curses. Now choose life, so that you and your children may live and that you may love the Lord your God, listen to his voice, and hold fast to him. For the Lord is your life, and he will give you many years in the land he swore to give to your fathers, Abraham, Isaac and Jacob. (Deuteronomy 30:19-20)

Passing on the Father's love
Find out what country your ancestors came from. Talk about the way of life

they experienced and how that compares to today.

☐ 222 _____

Whatever you do, work at it with all your heart, as working for the Lord, not for men, since you know that you will receive an inheritance from the Lord as a reward. It is the Lord Christ you are serving. (Colossians 3:23-24)

Passing on the Father's love
Take your child on a business trip or appointment. Let her know what you do for a living.

☐ 223 _____

Hallelujah! For our Lord God Almighty reigns. Let us rejoice and be glad and give him glory! For the wedding of the Lamb has come and his bride has made herself ready. (Revelation 19:6-7)

Passing on the Father's love
Take your children to a party, or have one at your house.

☐ 224 _____

Consider it pure joy, my brothers, whenever you face trials of many kinds, because you know that the testing of your faith develops perseverance. (James 1:2-3)

Passing on the Father's love

When you sense that your child has had a bad week, make time to go have some fun together.

A STRONG FINISH: Never promise something to a child and not give it to him, because in that way he learns to lie. The Talmud

☐ 225 _____

If you obey my commands, you will remain in my
love, just as I have obeyed my Father's commands
and remain in his love. I have told you this so that
my joy may be in you and that your joy may be
complete. (John 15:10-11)

> *Passing on the Father's love*
> **Have your children draw pictures or
> take notes about the subject of this Sun-
> day's sermon.**

☐ 226 _____

Because you are sons, God sent the Spirit of his
Son into our hearts, the Spirit who calls out,
"Abba, Father." (Galatians 4:6)

Passing on the Father's love

Discuss how God is a father to your children.

☐ 227 _____

God is not unjust; he will not forget your work and the love you have shown him as you have helped his people and continue to help them. (Hebrews 6:10)

Passing on the Father's love

Go on a grocery shopping trip with your children; then take the groceries to a local homeless shelter.

☐ 228 _____

The Lord God said, "It is not good for the man to be alone. I will make a helper suitable for him." (Genesis 2:18)

Passing on the Father's love

Invite your wife to join your fathering team by giving her a copy of *Beside Every Great Dad* by Ken Canfield and Nancy Swihart (Tyndale).

☐ 229 _____

That night the Lord appeared to him and said, "I am the God of your father Abraham. Do not be afraid, for I am with you." (Genesis 26:24)

Passing on the Father's love
Go with your child to his doctor's or dentist's appointment.

☐ 230 _____

I have seen his ways, but I will heal him; I will guide him and restore comfort to him. (Isaiah 57:18)

Passing on the Father's love
Talk about some of your children's friends whose parents have recently divorced.

☐ 231 _____

A good man leaves an inheritance for his children's children, but a sinner's wealth is stored up for the righteous. (Proverbs 13:22)

Passing on the Father's love
Decide who should be named guardian if both you and your wife are gone. Contact a lawyer and have your will drawn up if necessary.

A STRONG FINISH: Be aware of changes caused by your children growing older. Children have different needs and abilities at different ages.

WEEK 34

_____

In everything I did, I showed you that by this
kind of hard work we must help the weak,
remembering the words the Lord Jesus himself
said: "It is more blessed to give than to receive."
(Acts 20:35)

Passing on the Father's love

**Take your children to buy Christmas
gifts for a family whose father is in
prison. (Contact a ministry such as**

Prison Fellowship, which sponsors Operation Angel Tree.)

☐ 233 _____

As iron sharpens iron, so one man sharpens another. (Proverbs 27:17)

Passing on the Father's love
Model healthy male friendships by taking your son along next time you do something with other men.

☐ 234 _____

Jesus said, "Let the little children come to me, and do not hinder them, for the kingdom of heaven belongs to such as these." (Matthew 19:14)

Passing on the Father's love
Teach your children how to call home (collect).

☐ 235 _____

The people walking in darkness have seen a great light; on those living in the land of the shadow of death a light has dawned. (Isaiah 9:2)

Passing on the Father's love
Let your kids string up Christmas lights in their bedroom. Let them turn them on each night as they lie in bed.

I no longer call you servants, because a servant does not know his master's business. Instead, I have called you friends, for everything that I learned from my Father I have made known to you. You did not choose me, but I chose you and appointed you to go and bear fruit—fruit that will last. (John 15:15-16)

Passing on the Father's love
Call your child on the telephone, and tell her one exciting event of your day.

Whoever can be trusted with very little can also be trusted with much, and whoever is dishonest with very little will also be dishonest with much. So if you have not been trustworthy in handling worldly wealth, who will trust you with true riches? And if you have not been trustworthy with someone else's property, who will give you property of your own? (Luke 16:10-12)

Passing on the Father's love
Volunteer to be one of your child's club sponsors, leaders, or coaches.

"The share of the man who stayed with the supplies is to be the same as that of him who went down to the battle. All will share alike." David made this a statute and ordinance for Israel from that day to this. (1 Samuel 30:24-25)

Passing on the Father's love

Assign family chores that each child, however young, can be responsible for.

A STRONG FINISH: The best protection a father can provide for his children is to pray for them by name every day.

☐ 239 _____

The Lord is good, a refuge in times of trouble. He cares for those who trust in him, but with an overwhelming flood he will make an end of Nineveh; he will pursue his foes into darkness. (Nahum 1:7-8)

Passing on the Father's love
Demonstrate to your kids how to dial 9-1-1 and other emergency numbers.

☐ 240 _____

Let us not be like others, who are asleep, but let us be alert and self-controlled. For those who sleep, sleep at night, and those who get drunk, get drunk at night. But since we belong to the day, let us be self-controlled, putting on faith and love as a breastplate, and the hope of salvation as a helmet. (1 Thessalonians 5:6-8)

Passing on the Father's love
Design fire escape routes for each of your children in the house. Practice a fire drill, letting them sound the alarm or run the stopwatch.

☐ 241 _____

Do not store up for yourselves treasures on earth, where moth and rust destroy, and where thieves break in and steal. But store up for yourselves treasures in heaven, where moth and rust do not destroy, and where thieves do not break in and steal. For where your treasure is, there your heart will be also. (Matthew 6:19-21)

Passing on the Father's love
Sit down with your schedule and block out time to spend with your kids.

☐ 242 _____

Better is open rebuke than hidden love. Wounds from a friend can be trusted, but an enemy multiplies kisses. (Proverbs 27:5-6)

Passing on the Father's love
Ask someone who knows you well to suggest something you could do to

strengthen your relationship with your kids.

☐ 243 _____

Be sure you know the condition of your flocks, give careful attention to your herds; for riches do not endure forever, and a crown is not secure for all generations. (Proverbs 27:23-24)

Passing on the Father's love
If your teenager owns a car, wash it for him or her.

☐ 244 _____

The kingdom of heaven is like treasure hidden in a field. When a man found it, he hid it again, and then in his joy went and sold all he had and bought that field. Again, the kingdom of heaven is like a merchant looking for fine pearls. When he found one of great value, he went away and sold everything he had and bought it. (Matthew 13:44-46)

Passing on the Father's love
Ask your child what his or her most-prized possession is.

☐ 245 _____

Very early in the morning, while it was still dark, Jesus got up, left the house and went off to a solitary place, where he prayed. . . . Jesus often withdrew to lonely places and prayed.

(Mark 1:35; Luke 5:16)

Passing on the Father's love
Introduce your children to the spiritual discipline of solitude or fasting.

A STRONG FINISH: Bless our children, God, and help us so to fashion their souls by precept and example that they may ever love the good, flee from sin, revere thy word, and honor thy name.
Union Prayer Book

WEEK **36**

☐ 246 _____

No good tree bears bad fruit, nor does a bad tree bear good fruit. Each tree is recognized by its own fruit. People do not pick figs from thornbushes, or grapes from briers. The good man brings good things out of the good stored up in his heart, and the evil man brings evil things out of the evil stored up in his heart. (Luke 6:43-45)

Passing on the Father's love
Be sure to reward your child's proper attitudes as well as actions.

Then [Jacob] blessed Joseph and said, "May the God before whom my fathers Abraham and Isaac walked, the God who has been my shepherd all my life to this day, the Angel who has delivered me from all harm—may he bless these boys. May they be called by my name and the names of my fathers Abraham and Isaac, and may they increase greatly upon the earth." (Genesis 48:15-16)

Passing on the Father's love
Pray for each child before you leave for work by placing your hand on each of their heads.

□ 248 _____

At that time Jesus, full of joy through the Holy Spirit, said, "I praise you, Father, Lord of heaven and earth, because you have hidden these things from the wise and learned, and revealed them to little children. Yes, Father, for this was your good pleasure." (Luke 10:21)

Passing on the Father's love
Bring up a problem you've recently encountered at work; then ask your child, "How would you handle it?"

□ 249 _____

I will lead the blind by ways they have not known, along unfamiliar paths I will guide them; I will turn the darkness into light before them and make the rough places smooth. These are the things I will do; I will not forsake them. (Isaiah 42:16)

Passing on the Father's love
Go watch your child's sports, music, or play practice.

☐ 250 _____

So there was food every day for Elijah and for the woman and her family. For the jar of flour was not used up and the jug of oil did not run dry, in keeping with the word of the Lord spoken by Elijah. (1 Kings 17:15-16)

Passing on the Father's love
Let your children order at a restaurant.

☐ 251 _____

We are bringing you good news, telling you to turn from these worthless things to the living God, who made heaven and earth and sea and everything in them. . . . He has shown kindness by giving you rain from heaven and crops in their seasons; he provides you with plenty of food and fills your hearts with joy. (Acts 14:15, 17)

Passing on the Father's love
Think of the three best jokes or funny stories you've recently heard; then tell them during the dinner hour.

The fruit of the Spirit is love, joy, peace, patience, kindness, goodness, faithfulness, gentleness and self-control. Against such things there is no law. Those who belong to Christ Jesus have crucified the sinful nature with its passions and desires. Since we live by the Spirit, let us keep in step with the Spirit. Let us not become conceited, provoking and envying each other. (Galatians 5:22-26)

Passing on the Father's love
At the dinner table, tell each child one quality that you appreciate in him or her.

A STRONG FINISH: It is not enough for parents to understand children. They must accord children the privilege of understanding them. Milton R. Sapirstein

WEEK 37

☐ 253 _____

My people have been lost sheep; their shepherds have led them astray and caused them to roam on the mountains. They wandered over mountain and hill and forgot their own resting place. Whoever found them devoured them; their enemies said, "We are not guilty, for they sinned against the Lord, their true pasture, the Lord, the hope of their fathers." (Jeremiah 50:6-7)

If your children are old enough to handle such discussions, be bold and admit one of your major life mistakes.

☐ 254 _____

Now Isaac had come from Beer Lahai Roi, for he was living in the Negev. He went out to the field one evening to meditate, and as he looked up, he saw camels approaching. Rebekah also looked up and saw Isaac. She got down from her camel and asked the servant, "Who is that man in the field coming to meet us?" "He is my master," the servant answered. So she took her veil and covered herself. Then the servant told Isaac all he had done. Isaac brought her into the tent of his mother Sarah, and he married Rebekah. So she became his wife, and he loved her; and Isaac was comforted after his mother's death. (Genesis 24:62-67)

Passing on the Father's love

Tell your children why you decided to marry their mother.

☐ 255 _____

The woman said [to David], "Why then have you devised a thing like this against the people of God? When the king says this, does he not convict himself, for the king has not brought back his banished son? Like water spilled on the ground, which cannot be recovered, so we must die. But God does not take away life; instead, he devises ways so that a banished person may not remain estranged from him." . . . Then Joab went to Geshur and brought Absalom back to Jerusalem. (2 Samuel 14:13-14, 23)

Passing on the Father's love
Begin a reconciliation with your father by identifying his influence on you (both good and bad). List five ways you're like him and five ways you aren't.

☐ 256 _____

Do not lie to each other, since you have taken off your old self with its practices and have put on the new self, which is being renewed in knowledge in the image of its Creator. (Colossians 3:9-10)

Passing on the Father's love
Explain to your children why you consider lying to be wrong.

☐ 257 _____

Jesus spoke all these things to the crowd in parables; he did not say anything to them without using a parable. So was fulfilled what was spoken through the prophet: "I will open my mouth in parables, I will utter things hidden since the creation of the world." . . . With many similar parables Jesus spoke the word to them, as much as they could understand. (Matthew 13:34-35; Mark 4:33)

Passing on the Father's love
Watch a video with your child, and discuss it afterward.

☐ 258 _____

And Jesus grew in wisdom and stature, and in favor with God and men. (Luke 2:52)

Passing on the Father's love
Check out a book from the library on the stages of a child's growth.

☐ 259 _____

He unleashes his lightning beneath the whole heaven and sends it to the ends of the earth. After that comes the sound of his roar; he thunders with his majestic voice. When his voice resounds, he holds nothing back. God's voice thunders in marvelous ways; he does great things beyond our understanding. (Job 37:3-5)

Passing on the Father's love
During the next lightning storm, hold your child and look out the window together, remarking on the beauty of the flashes.

A STRONG FINISH: Helping children develop confidence prepares them for independence.

☐ 260 _____

God said to Jonah, "Do you have a right to be angry about the vine?" "I do," he said. "I am angry enough to die." But the Lord said, "You have been concerned about this vine, though you did not tend it or make it grow. It sprang up overnight and died overnight. But Nineveh has more than a hundred and twenty thousand people who cannot tell their right hand from their left, and many cattle as well. Should I not be concerned about that great city?" (Jonah 4:9-11)

Passing on the Father's love

After you discipline your children, find a time afterward when you affirm them for who they are.

☐ 261 _____

I will not take my love from him, nor will I ever betray my faithfulness. I will not violate my covenant or alter what my lips have uttered. Once for all, I have sworn by my holiness—and I will not lie to David. (Psalm 89:33-35)

Passing on the Father's love

Review in your mind what promises you have made to your kids lately that you still need to fulfill; make sure you keep them.

☐ 262 _____

Her husband has full confidence in her and lacks nothing of value. She brings him good, not harm, all the days of her life. She selects wool and flax and works with eager hands. She is like the merchant ships, bringing her food from afar. She gets up while it is still dark; she provides food for her family and portions for her servant girls. (Proverbs 31:11-15)

Passing on the Father's love

Identify ways that you can relieve some of the pressures your wife feels in her mothering.

☐ 263 _____

My salvation and my honor depend on God; he is my mighty rock, my refuge. Trust in him at all times, O people; pour out your hearts to him, for God is our refuge. (Psalm 62:7-8)

Passing on the Father's love
Discuss with your daughter what to expect on a date. Make sure you meet her date.

☐ 264 _____

Engrave the names of the sons of Israel on the two stones the way a gem cutter engraves a seal. Then mount the stones in gold filigree settings and fasten them on the shoulder pieces of the ephod as memorial stones for the sons of Israel. Aaron is to bear the names on his shoulders as a memorial before the Lord. (Exodus 28:11-12)

Passing on the Father's love
Ask for your children's school pictures to put in your wallet or on your office desk.

☐ 265 _____

Pray all the time. Ask God for anything in line with the Holy Spirit's wishes. Plead with him, reminding him of your needs, and keep praying earnestly for all Christians everywhere. (Ephesians 6:18, TLB)

Passing on the Father's love

Ask your kids if they have any complaints about "things at home." Let them air their feelings. Don't try to fix the situation. Ask them to suggest possible solutions if needed.

☐ 266 _____

To these four young men God gave knowledge and understanding of all kinds of literature and learning. And Daniel could understand visions and dreams of all kinds. . . . In every matter of wisdom and understanding about which the king questioned them, he found them ten times better than all the magicians and enchanters in his whole kingdom. (Daniel 1:17, 20)

Passing on the Father's love

Listen to your teenager's favorite music tape or CD. Ask her what she likes about the music.

A STRONG FINISH: In order to become skilled craftsmen as fathers, we must all begin as apprentices. We need to turn to other men and ask them, "Show me how you do this and do it well. What are your tricks of the trade?"

☐ 267 _____

The Lord will guide you always; he will satisfy your needs in a sun-scorched land and will strengthen your frame. You will be like a well-watered garden, like a spring whose waters never fail. (Isaiah 58:11)

Passing on the Father's love
Help your children memorize their address and phone number. Perhaps even have them learn a song with the numbers in it that they can sing to the police if they get lost.

☐ 268 _____

Blessed is the man who fears the Lord. . . . He will have no fear of bad news; his heart is steadfast, trusting in the Lord. His heart is secure, he will have no fear. (Psalm 112:1, 7-8)

Passing on the Father's love
Take your child to school on the first day of the new school year to help her feel secure.

☐ 269 _____

Deborah, a prophetess, the wife of Lappidoth, was leading Israel at that time. She held court under the Palm of Deborah between Ramah and Bethel in the hill country of Ephraim, and the Israelites came to her to have their disputes decided. (Judges 4:4-5)

Passing on the Father's love
Ask your wife what she thinks is your greatest strength as a father.

☐ 270 _____

Remember the days of old; consider the generations long past. Ask your father and he will tell you, your elders, and they will explain to you. (Deuteronomy 32:7)

Passing on the Father's love
Share with your kids one positive thing you received from your parents.

I know that there is nothing better for men than to be happy and do good while they live. That everyone may eat and drink, and find satisfaction in all his toil—this is the gift of God. (Ecclesiastes 3:12-13)

Passing on the Father's love
Tell your child, "Tomorrow is your day." Give him a budget and have him plan all the activities.

Then King Rehoboam consulted the elders who had served his father Solomon during his lifetime. "How would you advise me to answer these people?" he asked. . . . But Rehoboam rejected the advice the elders gave him and consulted the young men who had grown up with him and were serving him. . . . [He] answered the people harshly. (1 Kings 12:6, 8, 13)

Passing on the Father's love
Make a list of the men who support you in your fathering.

Flee the evil desires of youth, and pursue righteousness, faith, love and peace, along with those who call on the Lord out of a pure heart. Don't have anything to do with foolish and stupid arguments, because you know they produce quarrels. And the Lord's servant must not quarrel; instead, he must be kind to everyone, able to teach, not resentful. Those who oppose him he must gently instruct, in the hope that God will grant them repentance leading them to a knowledge of the truth, and that they will come to their senses and escape from the trap of the devil, who has taken them captive to do his will. (2 Timothy 2:22-26)

Passing on the Father's love

Ask your kids to tell you about one time when they successfully warded off an offer of drugs or alcohol. Show your pleasure at their wisdom.

A STRONG FINISH: The young need old men. They need men who are not ashamed of age, not pathetic imitations of themselves. Peter Ustinov

☐ 274 _____

In the same way, urge the young men to behave carefully, taking life seriously. And here you yourself must be an example to them of good deeds of every kind. (Titus 2:6-7, TLB)

Passing on the Father's love
Let your teenager drive you to church.

☐ 275 _____

But the Lord said to Samuel, "Do not consider his appearance or his height, for I have rejected him.

The Lord does not look at the things man looks at. Man looks at the outward appearance, but the Lord looks at the heart." (1 Samuel 16:7)

Passing on the Father's love

Talk to your children about who the most popular kids are at school and what makes them popular.

☐ 276 _____

For the fool speaks folly, his mind is busy with evil: He practices ungodliness and spreads error concerning the Lord; . . . The scoundrel's methods are wicked, he makes up evil schemes to destroy the poor with lies, even when the plea of the needy is just. But the noble man makes noble plans, and by noble deeds he stands. (Isaiah 32:6-8)

Passing on the Father's love

Set up a homework schedule for your child during a time when you're available to help. Take into consideration his or her need for exercise and fun, meals, family time, and household chores.

☐ 277 _____

Marriage should be honored by all, and the marriage bed kept pure, for God will judge the adulterer and all the sexually immoral. (Hebrews 13:4)

Write out your wedding vows and post them where your wife and children can read them.

☐ 278 _____

Now Jehoiada was old and full of years, and he died at the age of a hundred and thirty. He was buried with the kings in the City of David, because of the good he had done in Israel for God and his temple. (2 Chronicles 24:15-16)

Passing on the Father's love
If your parents are deceased, adopt an elderly couple as your children's grandparents.

☐ 279 _____

She is clothed with strength and dignity; she can laugh at the days to come. She speaks with wisdom, and faithful instruction is on her tongue. (Proverbs 31:25-26)

Passing on the Father's love
Compliment your daughter on a special quality you see in her.

☐ 280 _____

Abraham was the father of Isaac, Isaac the father of Jacob, . . . David was the father of Solomon, . . . and Jacob the father of Joseph, the husband of

Mary, of whom was born Jesus, who is called Christ. Thus there were fourteen generations in all from Abraham to David, fourteen from David to the exile to Babylon, and fourteen from the exile to the Christ. (Matthew 1:2, 6, 16-17)

Passing on the Father's love

Draw out a simple family history on a piece of paper. Fill in the names, with a characteristic about each person. Have your children add their own names to the list.

A STRONG FINISH: It is good for us to keep some account of our prayers, that we may not unsay them in our practice. Matthew Henry

Six Stages of Fathering

1. Attachment (0–1 years). From the moment your first child is conceived, you will begin to bond with your son or daughter. Your focus in life changes. You leave behind old routines, lose some sleep—and gain a new purpose.

2. Idealism (2–6 years). As a toddler grows and prepares to enter grade school, a father begins to develop a relationship with his child. During this stage you set your ideals and establish priorities concerning your fathering commitment.

3. Understanding (7–12 years). A father comes into his own—you can begin to introduce your child to the world: grade school, outside activities, like sports or clubs. But you leave behind simple ways of relating to your child and lose some control over what's influencing your child.

4. Enlightenment (13–18 years). A father may be going through his own midlife transition as his child is going through puberty; this generally leads to the lowest levels of fathering satisfaction during a father's life course.

Through active listening and staying involved, you can help your children and yourself negotiate this turbulent period.

5. Reflection (19–30 years). As their children become independent young adults, dads reflect on their efforts. Interestingly, children are often open to advice and help. Dads must be ready to pitch in as their children get firmly established.

6. Generativity (30 and over). Generativity means focusing on your contribution to the next generation—and a dad does this as his child has a child. Dads often find themselves relating in a new way to their grandchild when the pressures of being responsible and providing financially are lifted.

The National Center for fathering has a full range of resources for every father and fathering situation—new dads, fathers of teens, stepdads, divorced dads, granddads. Each of these resources features practical advice based on thorough research. Call or write us if you would like

- A free issue of our practical how-to oriented *Today's Father* magazine
- Books and tapes for every fathering situation
- Feedback on your fathering to help you identify your strengths and opportunities as a dad
- Seminars for your group or organization to raise the awareness of the importance of fathers and provide practical tips for improvement

- Materials for small groups to encourage and equip men in their fathering role

National Center for Fathering
800/593-3237

☐ 281 _____

At the end of every three years, bring all the tithes of that year's produce and store it in your towns, so that the . . . aliens, the fatherless and the widows who live in your towns may come and eat and be satisfied, and so that the Lord your God may bless you in all the work of your hands. (Deuteronomy 14:28-29)

Passing on the Father's love
Describe the ways you plan to care for your relatives. Help your kids visualize a family security system that is parallel to the Social Security system.

Flee from sexual immorality. All other sins a man commits are outside his body, but he who sins sexually sins against his own body. Do you not know that your body is a temple of the Holy Spirit, who is in you, whom you have received from God? You are not your own; you were bought at a price. Therefore honor God with your body. (1 Corinthians 6:18-20)

Passing on the Father's love
Give your son some guidelines and ideas for taking out a date. Then have him role-play it with his mother.

Do not use dishonest standards when measuring length, weight or quantity. Use honest scales and honest weights, an honest ephah and an honest hin. I am the Lord your God, who brought you out of Egypt. (Leviticus 19:35-36)

Passing on the Father's love
Open a discussion about cheating in school; help the children devise strategies to avoid the temptation.

Come, let us rebuild the wall of Jerusalem, and we will no longer be in disgrace. . . . Shallum son of Hallohesh, ruler of a half-district of Jerusalem, repaired the next section with the help of his daughters. (Nehemiah 2:17; 3:12)

Passing on the Father's love
Don't shy away from your teenage daughter; continue to give her appropriate physical signs of affection.

☐ 285 _____

All who are skilled among you are to come and make everything the Lord has commanded: the tabernacle with its tent and its covering, clasps, frames, crossbars, posts and bases; the ark with its poles and the atonement cover and the curtain that shields it; . . . the woven garments worn for ministering in the sanctuary. (Exodus 35:10-12, 19)

Passing on the Father's love
Bring home a souvenir from work for your kids to look at (reports, tools, computer paper, etc.). Describe how your work contributes to this product or service.

☐ 286 _____

May our Lord Jesus Christ himself and God our Father, who loved us and by his grace gave us eternal encouragement and good hope, encourage your hearts and strengthen you in every good deed and word. (2 Thessalonians 2:16-17)

Passing on the Father's love
Buy a blank greeting card for your child, and write an encouraging personal message.

Then those who feared the Lord talked with each other, and the Lord listened and heard. A scroll of remembrance was written in his presence concerning those who feared the Lord and honored his name. "They will be mine," says the Lord Almighty, "in the day when I make up my treasured possession. I will spare them, just as in compassion a man spares his son who serves him. And you will again see the distinction between the righteous and the wicked, between those who serve God and those who do not." (Malachi 3:16-18)

Passing on the Father's love
Show your children the family scrapbook or some family mementos. Talk about specific articles and what they mean.

A STRONG FINISH: The faithful father is loyal. He says, "My kids are a priority," even in the face of all the pressures and expectations the world places upon him.

☐ 288 _____

Let him kiss me with the kisses of his mouth—for
your love is more delightful than wine. Pleasing is
the fragrance of your perfumes; your name is like
perfume poured out. No wonder the maidens love
you! (Song of Songs 1:2-3)

Passing on the Father's love
**Come home and kiss your wife in your
kids' sight.**

☐ 289 _____

At the end of the ten days [Daniel and his friends]
looked healthier and better nourished than any of
the young men who ate the royal food. . . . To
these four young men God gave knowledge and

understanding of all kinds of literature and learning. And Daniel could understand visions and dreams of all kinds. (Daniel 1:15, 17)

Passing on the Father's love

Point out to your adolescent son signs you see of him growing into a man.

☐ 290 _____

When Solomon had finished all these prayers and supplications to the Lord, he rose from before the altar of the Lord, where he had been kneeling with his hands spread out toward heaven. He stood and blessed the whole assembly of Israel in a loud voice, saying: "Praise be to the Lord, who has given rest to his people Israel just as he promised." (1 Kings 8:54-56)

Passing on the Father's love

Listen to your children as they pray; teach them different aspects of prayer: worship, thanksgiving, petition for ourselves, and intercession for others.

☐ 291 _____

A student is not above his teacher, but everyone who is fully trained will be like his teacher. (Luke 6:40)

Passing on the Father's love

Ask your children to describe their teacher(s) to you. What do they like or dislike about them?

So I made up my mind that I would not make another painful visit to you. For if I grieve you, who is left to make me glad but you whom I have grieved? I wrote as I did so that when I came I should not be distressed by those who ought to make me rejoice. I had confidence in all of you, that you would all share my joy. For I wrote you out of great distress and anguish of heart and with many tears, not to grieve you but to let you know the depth of my love for you. (2 Corinthians 2:1-4)

Passing on the Father's love
If there is something you've done that has caused your kids pain and you are unable to talk to them about it, write a letter in which you apologize and tell them how much you want to do better in the future.

When the time drew near for David to die, he gave a charge to Solomon his son. "I am about to go the way of all the earth," he said. "So be strong, show yourself a man, and observe what the Lord your God requires: Walk in his ways, and keep his decrees and commands, his laws and requirements, as written in the Law of Moses, so that you may prosper in all you do and wherever you go, and that the Lord may keep his promise to me." (1 Kings 2:1-4)

Passing on the Father's love
Spend a day at college with your child. Eat in the cafeteria; attend some of his classes.

☐ 294 _____

When they had seen him, they spread the word concerning what had been told them about this child, and all who heard it were amazed at what the shepherds said to them. But Mary treasured up all these things and pondered them in her heart. (Luke 2:17-19)

Passing on the Father's love
Get out your kids' baby pictures, and tell them stories about what they were like as babies.

A STRONG FINISH: Realize early on that you are only stewards of your children. Treat them as you would want your grandchildren treated.

☐ 295 _____

For the Lord is always good. He is always loving and kind, and his faithfulness goes on and on to each succeeding generation. (Psalm 100:5, TLB)

Passing on the Father's love
Tell your kids, "I love you," even if you have already said so twice this year.

☐ 296 _____

Declare a holy fast; call a sacred assembly. Summon the elders and all who live in the land to the house

of the Lord your God and cry out to the Lord. . . .
To you, O Lord, I call, for fire has devoured the
open pastures and flames have burned up all the
trees of the field. (Joel 1:14, 19)

Passing on the Father's love
**Make times of family crisis times of fam-
ily discussion. Let your children hear
what you are thinking and feeling. Let
them say what they need to say.**

□ 297 _____

Hilkiah the priest found the Book of the Law of the
Lord that had been given through Moses. . . . Then
Shaphan took the book to the king and reported to
him: . . . "Hilkiah the priest has given me a book."
And Shaphan read from it in the presence of the
king. When the king heard the words of the Law, he
tore his robes. He gave these orders: . . . "Go and
inquire of the Lord for me and for the remnant in
Israel and Judah about what is written in this book
that has been found. Great is the Lord's anger that
is poured out on us because our fathers have not
kept the word of the Lord; they have not acted in
accordance with all that is written in this book."
(2 Chronicles 34:14-21)

Passing on the Father's love
**Take your children to the library, and
give them thirty minutes to browse and
check out some books.**

When Israel saw the sons of Joseph, he asked,
"Who are these?" "They are the sons God has given
me here," Joseph said to his father. . . . Israel said
to Joseph, "I never expected to see your face again,
and now God has allowed me to see your children
too." (Genesis 48:8-9, 11)

Passing on the Father's love

**Take a picture of your child and her
friends when the friends are over to play.**

I have revealed you to those whom you gave me
out of the world. They were yours; you gave them
to me. . . . I pray for them. I am not praying for
the world, but for those you have given me, for
they are yours. . . . Holy Father, protect them by
the power of your name . . . so that they may be
one as we are one. . . . My prayer is not that you
take them out of the world but that you protect
them from the evil one. (John 17:6-15)

Passing on the Father's love

**Skip lunch today. Fast and pray for your
children.**

But a Samaritan, as he traveled, came where the
man was; and when he saw him, he took pity on
him. He went to him and bandaged his wounds,

pouring on oil and wine. Then he put the man on his own donkey, took him to an inn and took care of him. (Luke 10:33-34)

Passing on the Father's love
Participate in the nitty-gritty of your child's life by giving a bath, changing a diaper, or helping with homework.

☐ 301 _____

Then Rachel said, "God has vindicated me; he has listened to my plea and given me a son." Because of this she named him Dan. (Genesis 30:6)

Passing on the Father's love
Make an acrostic with your child's name, where each letter stands for a positive quality. Hang it on his or her bedroom door.

A STRONG FINISH: The best portion of a good man's life is his little, nameless, unremembered acts of kindness and of love. William Wordsworth

☐ 302 _____

When others are happy, be happy with them. If they are sad, share their sorrow. (Romans 12:15, TLB)

Passing on the Father's love
When your daughter or son starts to cry, make sure you provide the tissue to wipe away the tears. Then be still and listen.

☐ 303 _____

So if you are standing before the altar in the Temple, offering a sacrifice to God, and suddenly remember that a friend has something against you, leave your sacrifice there beside the altar and go and apologize and be reconciled to him, and then come and offer your sacrifice to God. (Matthew 5:23-24, TLB)

Passing on the Father's love
Ask your children if there is anything for which you need to ask forgiveness.

☐ 304 _____

Not many of you should presume to be teachers, my brothers, because you know that we who teach will be judged more strictly. We all stumble in many ways. If anyone is never at fault in what he says, he is a perfect man, able to keep his whole body in check. (James 3:1-2)

Passing on the Father's love
Tell your children a story about your all-time favorite teacher. Make sure you express why you liked that person and what you learned from him or her.

☐ 305 _____

On this mountain the Lord Almighty will prepare a feast of rich food for all peoples, a banquet of aged wine—the best of meats and the finest of wines. On this mountain he will destroy the shroud that enfolds all peoples, the sheet that covers all nations; he will swallow up death forever. The Sovereign Lord will wipe away the tears from all faces; he will remove the disgrace of his people from all the earth. The Lord has spoken. (Isaiah 25:6-8)

Passing on the Father's love
Invite one of your children's friends over for dinner.

☐ 306 _____

Therefore I am now going to allure her; I will lead her into the desert and speak tenderly to her. There I will give her back her vineyards, and will make the Valley of Achor a door of hope. There she will sing as in the days of her youth. (Hosea 2:14-15)

Passing on the Father's love
Arrange for someone else to take care of the kids while you and your wife spend an entire weekend alone together.

☐ 307 _____

And this is my prayer: that your love may abound more and more in knowledge and depth of insight, so that you may be able to discern what is best and may be pure and blameless until the day of Christ. (Philippians 1:9-10)

Passing on the Father's love
Go to a movie of your children's choosing. Afterward discuss the plot and scenes. Ask them what they liked best about the movie.

Suppose one of you wants to build a tower. Will he not first sit down and estimate the cost to see if he has enough money to complete it? (Luke 14:28)

Passing on the Father's love
Help your kids set up a budget applicable to them.

A STRONG FINISH: If you don't respect your parents, your child will not respect you. Maimonides

☐ 309 _____

If it is possible, as far as it depends on you, live at peace with everyone. . . . Let us therefore make every effort to do what leads to peace and to mutual edification. (Romans 12:18; 14:19)

Passing on the Father's love
Help your child figure out how to deal with a problem relationship in their circle, whether at school, in the neighborhood, or within the church.

☐ 310 _____

Let Israel rejoice in their Maker; let the people of Zion be glad in their King. Let them praise his name with dancing and make music to him with tambourine and harp. For the Lord takes delight in his people; he crowns the humble with salvation. (Psalm 149:2-4)

Passing on the Father's love

Frame and mount a piece of your child's artwork.

☐ 311 _____

Dear friends, this is now my second letter to you. I have written both of them as reminders to stimulate you to wholesome thinking. I want you to recall the words spoken in the past by the holy prophets and the command given by our Lord and Savior through your apostles. (2 Peter 3:1-2)

Passing on the Father's love

Write a letter to your child in college, even if you have no big news to tell.

☐ 312 _____

Quietly trust yourself to Christ your Lord, and if anybody asks why you believe as you do, be ready to tell him, and do it in a gentle and respectful way. (1 Peter 3:15, TLB)

Passing on the Father's love

Ask your child what her friends believe about God.

Enlarge the place of your tent, stretch your tent curtains wide, do not hold back; lengthen your cords, strengthen your stakes. For you will spread out to the right and to the left. (Isaiah 54:2-3)

Passing on the Father's love
Take your child to a place that's special for you and your wife. Explain its significance and add that now it's even better.

Let me understand the teaching of your precepts; then I will meditate on your wonders. My soul is weary with sorrow; strengthen me according to your word. (Psalm 119:27-28)

Passing on the Father's love
Search the Scriptures with your child for a verse that applies to a struggle she is going through.

Do you want to be truly rich? You already are if you are happy and good. After all, we didn't bring any money with us when we came into the world, and we can't carry away a single penny when we die. (1 Timothy 6:6-7, TLB)

Passing on the Father's love
Teach your older children how to write a check and balance a checkbook.

A STRONG FINISH: A father's system of discipline is really only a smaller part of a more important item, the father's belief system and perspective.

☐ 316 _____

When Elizabeth heard Mary's greeting, the baby leaped in her womb, and Elizabeth was filled with the Holy Spirit. . . . "As soon as the sound of your greeting reached my ears, the baby in my womb leaped for joy. Blessed is she who has believed that what the Lord has said to her will be accomplished!" (Luke 1:41, 44-45)

Passing on the Father's love
Have each of the kids make Christmas cards to give to other family members.

On the Lord's Day I was in the Spirit, and I heard behind me a loud voice like a trumpet, which said: "Write on a scroll what you see and send it to the seven churches: . . . Write, therefore, what you have seen, what is now and what will take place later. The mystery of the seven stars that you saw in my right hand and of the seven golden lampstands is this: The seven stars are the angels of the seven churches, and the seven lampstands are the seven churches. (Revelation 1:10-11, 19-20)

Passing on the Father's love
Read a book or short story to your child tonight. Include her and yourself in the plot.

Listen, my sons, to a father's instruction; pay attention and gain understanding. (Proverbs 4:1)

Passing on the Father's love
Reverse roles with your son or daughter, with child teaching parent some skill or information.

Your beauty should not come from outward adornment, such as braided hair and the wearing of gold jewelry and fine clothes. Instead, it should be that of your inner self, the unfading beauty of a gentle and quiet spirit, which is of great worth in God's sight. (1 Peter 3:3-4)

Passing on the Father's love

Tell your daughter that she is beautiful inwardly and outwardly. Give her some specific examples of that beauty.

☐ 320 _____

Jacob and all the people with him came to Luz (that is, Bethel) in the land of Canaan. There he built an altar, and he called the place El Bethel, because it was there that God revealed himself to him when he was fleeing from his brother. (Genesis 35:6-7)

Passing on the Father's love

When you visit your child at college, ask him if he has discovered an interesting place, and have him take you there.

☐ 321 _____

It is written in the Prophets: 'They will all be taught by God.' Everyone who listens to the Father and learns from him comes to me. (John 6:45)

Passing on the Father's love

As you pray today, include the request: "Heavenly Father, show me what type of father you are."

The Lord is full of compassion and mercy. (James 5:11)

Passing on the Father's love

Give each of your children a big hug today.

A STRONG FINISH: The man will never be unwelcome to others who makes himself agreeable to his own family. Plautus

☐ 323 _____

Now the Lord was gracious to Sarah as he had said,
and the Lord did for Sarah what he had promised.
Sarah became pregnant and bore a son to Abraham in
his old age, at the very time God had promised
him. . . . Sarah said, "God has brought me laughter,
and everyone who hears about this will laugh with
me." And she added, "Who would have said to Abraham that Sarah would nurse children? Yet I have borne
him a son in his old age." (Genesis 21:1-2, 6-7)

Describe the events surrounding your children's births.

☐ 324 _____

O great and powerful God, whose name is the Lord Almighty, great are your purposes and mighty are your deeds. Your eyes are open to all the ways of men; you reward everyone according to his conduct and as his deeds deserve. (Jeremiah 32:18-19)

Passing on the Father's love
Be a chaperone at the next school function.

☐ 325 _____

David son of Jesse was king over all Israel. He ruled over Israel forty years. . . . He died at a good old age, having enjoyed long life, wealth and honor. His son Solomon succeeded him as king. (1 Chronicles 29:26-28)

Passing on the Father's love
Tell your children something you have come to appreciate about your parents.

☐ 326 _____

David said to Saul, "Let no one lose heart on account of this Philistine; your servant will go and fight him." Saul replied, "You are not able to go out against this Philistine and fight him; you are only a boy, and he has been a fighting man from his youth." But David said to Saul, "Your servant has killed both the lion and the bear; this uncircumcised Philistine will be like one of them, because he has defied the armies of the living God. The Lord who delivered me from the paw of the lion and the paw of the bear will deliver me from the hand of this Philistine." (1 Samuel 17:32-34, 36-37)

Passing on the Father's love
Praise your child when you see improvement in his or her athletic abilities.

☐ 327 _____

Her children arise and call her blessed; her husband also, and he praises her: "Many women do noble things, but you surpass them all." (Proverbs 31:28-29)

Passing on the Father's love
Take your kids Christmas shopping for their mother; help them out financially if need be.

☐ 328 _____

Timothy, you are like a son to me in the things of the Lord. May God our Father and Jesus Christ our Lord show you his kindness and mercy and give you great peace of heart and mind. . . . Now, Timothy, my son, here is my command to you: Fight well in the Lord's battles, just as the Lord told us through his prophets that you would. (1 Timothy 1:2, 18, TLB)

Tell your older children the one thing you are going to miss most about them when they eventually move out of the house.

☐ 329 _____

Build homes and plan to stay; plant vineyards, for you will be there many years. Marry and have children, and then find mates for them and have many grandchildren. Multiply! Don't dwindle away! And work for the peace and prosperity of Babylon. Pray for her, for if Babylon has peace, so will you. (Jeremiah 29:5-7, TLB)

Passing on the Father's love
Show your children pictures of you and your wife when you were kids.

A STRONG FINISH: Making memories with your children is like putting money into a savings account.

☐ 330 _____

Although the Lord gives you the bread of adversity and the water of affliction, your teachers will be hidden no more; with your own eyes you will see them. Whether you turn to the right or to the left, your ears will hear a voice behind you, saying, "This is the way; walk in it." (Isaiah 30:20-21)

Passing on the Father's love
Call your child's teacher, and ask how your child is doing.

We know and rely on the love God has for us. God is love. Whoever lives in love lives in God, and God in him. In this way, love is made complete among us so that we will have confidence on the day of judgment, because in this world we are like him. There is no fear in love. But perfect love drives out fear, because fear has to do with punishment. . . . We love because he first loved us. (1 John 4:16-19)

Passing on the Father's love
Tell your children you love them for who they are, not for what you hope they will be. Give some specific examples.

For wisdom and truth will enter the very center of your being, filling your life with joy. You will be given the sense to stay away from evil men who want you to be their partners in crime—men who turn from God's ways to walk down dark and evil paths. (Proverbs 2:10-13, TLB)

Passing on the Father's love
Ask your child about the new friends he has made at school this year.

When Joseph woke up, he did what the angel of the Lord had commanded him and took Mary home as his wife. But he had no union with her until she gave birth to a son. And he gave him the name Jesus. (Matthew 1:24-25)

Passing on the Father's love

Take pictures of your kids today. Begin a personal photo album for each child.

☐ 334 _____

I have not sent these prophets, yet they claim to speak for me; I gave them no message, yet they say their words are mine. If they were mine, they would try to turn my people from their evil ways. (Jeremiah 23:21-22, TLB)

Passing on the Father's love

Help your high schooler research prospective colleges. Send off for catalogs.

☐ 335 _____

But I tell you who hear me: Love your enemies, do good to those who hate you, bless those who curse you, pray for those who mistreat you. . . . Then your reward will be great, and you will be sons of the Most High, because he is kind to the ungrateful and wicked. Be merciful, just as your Father is merciful. (Luke 6:27-28, 35-36)

Passing on the Father's love

Watch a TV show with your child, and discuss the good or bad ethics presented in the show.

O God, you have helped me from my earliest child-hood—and I have constantly testified to others of the wonderful things you do. And now that I am old and gray, don't forsake me. Give me time to tell this new generation (and their children too) about all your mighty miracles. Your power and goodness, Lord, reach to the highest heavens. You have done such wonderful things. Where is there another God like you? (Psalm 71:17-19, TLB)

Passing on the Father's love
Help your kids sketch out their family tree on paper.

A STRONG FINISH: The test of real fatherhood is not to try to be the ultimate father, but to point to the real One from whom reality comes.
Don Osgood

☐ 337 _____

When the builders completed the foundation of the Temple, the priests put on their official robes and blew their trumpets; and the descendants of Asaph crashed their cymbals to praise the Lord in the manner ordained by King David. They sang rounds of praise and thanks to God, singing this song: "He is good, and his love and mercy toward Israel will last forever." Then all the people gave a great shout, praising

God because the foundation of the Temple had been laid. (Ezra 3:10-11, TLB)

Passing on the Father's love
Ask your kids what new, unique Christmas traditions they would like to start.

□ 338 _____

Paul and Barnabas argued and discussed this with them at length, and finally the believers sent them to Jerusalem, accompanied by some local men, to talk to the apostles and elders there about this question. (Acts 15:2, TLB)

Passing on the Father's love
Discuss an area in which you and your child disagree. Listen.

□ 339 _____

Behold, a virgin shall be with child, and shall bring forth a son, and they shall call his name Emmanuel . . . God with us. (Matthew 1:23, KJV)

Passing on the Father's love
Tell your kids your favorite Christmas memory.

□ 340 _____

The lips of the righteous know what is fitting, but the mouth of the wicked only what is perverse. (Proverbs 10:32)

Learn what you can tease your kids about, and what subjects they are sensitive to.

☐ 341 _____

I commend you to our sister Phoebe, a servant of the church in Cenchrea. I ask you to receive her in the Lord in a way worthy of the saints and to give her any help she may need from you, for she has been a great help to many people, including me. . . . Greet Mary, who worked very hard for you. . . . . Greet Tryphena and Tryphosa, those women who work hard in the Lord. Greet my dear friend Persis, another woman who has worked very hard in the Lord. (Romans 16:1-2, 6, 12)

Passing on the Father's love
Ask your daughter what she likes to do with you, and set a date to do that together.

☐ 342 _____

The Lord called Samuel a third time, and Samuel got up and went to Eli and said, "Here I am; you called me." Then Eli realized that the Lord was calling the boy. So Eli told Samuel, "Go and lie down, and if he calls you, say, 'Speak, Lord, for your servant is listening.'" (1 Samuel 3:8-9)

Passing on the Father's love
Ask your older children for advice on a particular subject.

☐ 343 _____

My beloved said to me, "Rise up, my love, my fair one, and come away. For the winter is past, the rain is over and gone. The flowers are springing up and the time of the singing of birds has come. Yes, spring is here. The leaves are coming out, and the grapevines are in blossom. How delicious they smell! Arise, my love, my fair one, and come away." (Song of Solomon 2:10-13, TLB)

Passing on the Father's love
Bring home a card and flowers for your wife.

A STRONG FINISH: Your child may have his own best friend, but you need to be your child's best fan!

□ 344 _____

[Anna] was very old; she . . . was a widow until she
was eighty-four. . . . Coming up to them at that
very moment, she gave thanks to God and spoke
about the child to all who were looking forward to
the redemption. (Luke 2:36-38)

Passing on the Father's love
**Go with another family to sing Christmas
carols at a nursing home.**

□ 345 _____

And how can we be sure that we belong to him? By
looking within ourselves: are we really trying to do

what he wants us to? . . . Those who do what Christ tells them to will learn to love God more and more. . . . Anyone who says he is a Christian should live as Christ did. (1 John 2:3, 5-6, TLB)

Passing on the Father's love
Think of a mistake you have made as a father; then humbly share it with another man who will give you encouragement and support.

☐ 346 _____

And there were shepherds living out in the fields nearby, keeping watch over their flocks at night. An angel of the Lord appeared to them, and the glory of the Lord shone around them, and they were terrified. But the angel said to them, "Do not be afraid. I bring you good news of great joy that will be for all the people. Today in the town of David a Savior has been born to you; he is Christ the Lord. This will be a sign to you: You will find a baby wrapped in cloths and lying in a manger." Suddenly a great company of the heavenly host appeared with the angel, praising God and saying, "Glory to God in the highest, and on earth peace to men on whom his favor rests." (Luke 2:8-14)

Passing on the Father's love
Drive around as a family and look at the holiday lights.

_____

Each man should give what he has decided in his heart to give, not reluctantly or under compulsion, for God loves a cheerful giver. And God is able to make all grace abound to you, so that in all things at all times, having all that you need, you will abound in every good work. As it is written: "He has scattered abroad his gifts to the poor; his righteousness endures forever." (2 Corinthians 9:7-9)

Passing on the Father's love
Talk to your child about setting aside a percentage of her "income" for charity, and then help her find a kid-related church or community project.

_____

When I was a child, I talked like a child, I thought like a child, I reasoned like a child. When I became a man, I put childish ways behind me. (1 Corinthians 13:11)

Passing on the Father's love
Make Santa Claus an enjoyable pretend *game*; you don't need to claim he's real. In fact, you can present the historical Saint Nicholas—he was quite a man. (See *People Whose Faith Got Them into Trouble* by John Cowart [IVP].)

_____

When the king's order and edict had been proclaimed, many girls were brought to the citadel of

Susa and put under the care of Hegai. Esther also was taken to the king's palace and entrusted to Hegai. . . . The girl pleased him and won his favor. Immediately he provided her with her beauty treatments and special food. He assigned to her seven maids selected from the king's palace. (Esther 2:8-9)

Passing on the Father's love
Buy your daughter a subscription to her favorite magazine.

☐ 350 _____

After this, Paul left Athens and went to Corinth. There he met a Jew named Aquila, a native of Pontus, who had recently come from Italy with his wife Priscilla, because Claudius had ordered all the Jews to leave Rome. Paul went to see them, and because he was a tentmaker as they were, he stayed and worked with them. (Acts 18:1-3)

Passing on the Father's love
Let your children enjoy some of the dignity of what you do. Write them a letter on official stationery if you have some available.

A STRONG FINISH: Listening is a foundational discipline for fathering activities, and it is important because it feeds all our other fathering roles.

Just for Laughs!

Before I got married I had six theories about bringing up children; now I have six children and no theories.
Lord Rochester

Children are a great comfort in your old age—and they help you reach it faster, too. L. Kaufman

You know your little girl has grown up when she can hold a boy at arm's length without losing her grip on him.
Anonymous

A father is a fellow who has replaced the currency in his wallet with snapshots of his kids. Mike Forest

You know children are growing up when they start asking questions that have answers. J. J. Plomp

I pray, not for the remission of my sins, but the wit to remember them when they come back to me as my offspring's.
W. Gibson

A family starts with a young man falling in love with a girl—no superior alternative has yet been found. Winston Churchill

One of life's greatest mysteries is how the boy who wasn't good enough to marry your daughter can be the father of the smartest grandchild in the world.
Anonymous

This would be a better world for children if parents had to eat spinach. Groucho Marx

Children are unpredictable. You never know what inconsistency they're going to catch you in next. F. P. Jones

☐ 351 _____

And a voice from heaven said, "This is my son, whom I love; with him I am well pleased." (Matthew 3:17)

Passing on the Father's love
Give a wink or an approving nod with a smile to your child.

☐ 352 _____

For he himself is our peace, who has made the two one and has destroyed the barrier, the dividing wall of hostility, by abolishing in his flesh the law with its commandments and regulations. His purpose was to create in himself one new man out of the two, thus making peace, and in this one body to reconcile both of them to God through the cross, by which he put to death their hostility. He came and preached peace to you who were far away and peace to those who were near. For through him we both have access to the Father by one spirit. (Ephesians 2:14-18)

Passing on the Father's love
Expose your children to other cultures by inviting ethnic and international friends to your home.

☐ 353 _____

But the angel said to them, "Do not be afraid. I bring you good news of great joy that will be for all the people." (Luke 2:10)

Passing on the Father's love
Invite an international family over to experience the meaning of Christmas with your family.

☐ 354 _____

And when they were come into the house, they saw the young child with Mary his mother, and fell down, and worshipped him. (Matthew 2:11, KJV)

Passing on the Father's love
Light candles and read the Christmas story.

☐ 355 _____

I will lead them beside streams of water on a level path where they will not stumble, because I am Israel's father, and Ephraim is my firstborn son. (Jeremiah 31:9)

Passing on the Father's love
Ask your kids to describe a good father; then you describe a good son or daughter.

☐ 356 _____

Let them give thanks to the Lord for his unfailing love and his wonderful deeds for men, for he satisfies the thirsty and fills the hungry with good things. (Psalm 107:8-9)

Passing on the Father's love
Bake cookies with your kids; then go pass them out in your neighborhood.

☐ 357 _____

Be imitators of God, therefore, as dearly loved children and live a life of love, just as Christ loved us and gave himself up for us as a fragrant offering and sacrifice to God. (Ephesians 5:1-2)

Passing on the Father's love
Tell your children some sacrifice you have made in order to become an effective father.

A STRONG FINISH: Our children are likely to live up to what we believe of them. L. B. Johnson

WEEK **52**

☐ 358 _____

You gave me life and showed me kindness, and in your providence watched over my spirit. (Job 10:12)

Passing on the Father's love
Find out if there are any fathering seminars in your area and make plans to attend one in the coming year.

☐ 359 _____

Praise be to the God and Father of our Lord Jesus Christ, who has blessed us in the heavenly realms with every spiritual blessing in Christ. For he chose us in him before the creation of the world to be holy and blameless in his sight. In love he predestined us to be adopted as his sons through Jesus Christ, in accordance with his pleasure and will—to the praise of his glorious grace, which he has freely given us in the One he loves. (Ephesians 1:3-6)

Passing on the Father's love
Explain to your children how God has adopted them into his kingdom as sons and daughters.

☐ 360 _____

And Joshua set up at Gilgal the twelve stones they had taken out of the Jordan. He said to the Israelites, "In the future when your descendants ask their fathers, 'What do these stones mean?' tell them, 'Israel crossed the Jordan on dry ground.' For the Lord your God dried up the Jordan before you until you had crossed over. . . . He did this so that all the peoples of the earth might know that the hand of the Lord is powerful and so that you might always fear the Lord your God." (Joshua 4:20-24)

Passing on the Father's love
Write up a quiz that asks questions concerning the past year's activities, memories, or developments. Fix a snack and share your answers.

☐ 361 _____

[Jesus] got up from the meal, took off his outer
clothing, and wrapped a towel around his waist.
After that, he poured water into a basin and began
to wash his disciples' feet, drying them with the
towel that was wrapped around him. (John 13:4-5)

Passing on the Father's love
**Don't make your wife eat a cold dinner
tonight because she's busy meeting everyone else's demands. You jump up and
serve her and your family at dinner.**

☐ 362 _____

We also rejoice in our sufferings, because we know
that suffering produces perseverance; perseverance, character, and character, hope. And hope
does not disappoint us, because God has poured
out his love into our hearts by the Holy Spirit,
whom he has given us. (Romans 5:3-5)

Passing on the Father's love
**Ask your child what was his biggest dis-
appointment this year.**

☐ 363 _____

For I know your eagerness to help, and I have been
boasting about it to the Macedonians, telling them
that since last year you in Achaia were ready to
give; and your enthusiasm has stirred most of them
to action. . . . So I thought it necessary to urge the

brothers to visit you in advance and finish the arrangements for the generous gift you had promised. Then it will be ready as a generous gift, not as one grudgingly given. (2 Corinthians 9:2, 5)

Passing on the Father's love
Encourage your children to lay money aside for the offering plate at church.

☐ 364 _____

The prayer of a righteous man is powerful and effective. (James 5:16)

Passing on the Father's love
Pray daily for each of your children by name.

A STRONG FINISH: We never know the love of a parent till we become parents ourselves. When we first bend over the cradle of our own child, God throws back the temple door, and reveals to us the sacredness and mystery of a father's and a mother's love to ourselves. Henry Ward Beecher

☐ 365 _____

Count off seven weeks from the time you begin to put the sickle to the standing grain. Then celebrate the Feast of Weeks to the Lord your God by giving a freewill offering in proportion to the blessings the Lord your God has given you. And rejoice before the Lord your God at the place he will choose as a dwelling for his Name—you, your sons and daughters, your menservants and maid-servants, the Levites in your towns, and the aliens, the fatherless and the widows living among you. (Deuteronomy 16:9-11)

Passing on the Father's love

Stay up with your kids till midnight and count down the seconds till the New Year.

What Kids Say about Their Dads

The best thing about my dad is that he loves my mom so much they won't get divorced. A first grader

When I feel loved by a man, really loved and cherished, it is very much like the feeling of love I used to have with my father. Jessica, 25, in *Like Father, Like Daughter*

My dad loves me no matter what I do. When I lie, make big mistakes, or even break something, he still loves me. A third grader

My dad is the type of guy that you can talk to about school, other boys, or just plain girlfriends. A seventh grader

My dad is a Frito-Lay man. That is an important job. Because Frito-Lay means chips which is food. That is so important

because you could not live without food.
A first grader

My dad makes fun food, like Malt-O-Meal
and then dyes it green and says it's
because of grasshopper guts or something like that. A kindergartner

When I sit in his lap, it warms my whole
body inside and out. A seventh grader

Last year people asked him to be mayor
and he said, "No, I'm going to spend more
time with my kids." That's why he is the
best dad. A third grader

My dad is a guy who, when you are on a
dirt road, likes to swerve around and
make Mom say, "Kenneth!" He likes to
tease us, and he likes to laugh. A sixth
grader

My father's most influential moments
were the inadvertent ones. Not the times
when he was trying to tell me what life
was about. But those times when he
showed me how to live. A young adult, in
The Caring Father

I feel that if there were a vote on who to give an award I would vote for the fathers. A third grader

You probably were happy when I was born. I really would like to thank you for helping Mom have me. A third grader

They spend time together without us, like they will go out on what they call a date, and we can't go. But we do not mind . . . because if you could see Papa and Mama together, you would feel good too. A child, quoted in *A Dad Is for Spending Time With*

Without my father it would be like a ball without any air inside it. A sixth grader

APPENDIX

Holidays
throughout
the Year
arranged
alphabetically

☐ Advent (season) _____

But you, Bethlehem Ephrathah, though you are
small among the clans of Judah, out of you will
come for me one who will be ruler over Israel,
whose origins are from of old, from ancient
times. . . . He will stand and shepherd his flock in
the strength of the Lord, in the majesty of the
name of the Lord his God. And they will live
securely, for then his greatness will reach to the
ends of the earth. And he will be their peace.
(Micah 5:2-5)

Passing on the Father's love
**Plan several small events between now
and Christmas, to help the entire family
celebrate the anticipation of Jesus' birth.**

☐ All Saints' Day (November 1) _____

Therefore, since we are surrounded by such a great
cloud of witnesses, let us throw off everything that
hinders and the sin that so easily entangles, and let

us run with perseverance the race marked out for us. Let us fix our eyes on Jesus, the author and perfecter of our faith, who for the joy set before him endured the cross, scorning its shame, and sat down at the right hand of the throne of God. (Hebrews 12:1-2)

Passing on the Father's love

Make a family memorial display, using pictures, greeting cards, church bulletins, letters, etc., that tell something about saints your family admires. "Saints" can be historical figures, from the Bible or church history, or people of faith in present or recent times who have had a positive impact on your family.

☐ American Indian Day (4th Friday in September) _____

From one man he made every nation of men, that they should inhabit the whole earth; and he determined the times set for them and the exact places where they should live. God did this so that men would seek him and perhaps reach out for him and find him, though he is not far from each one of us. (Acts 17:26-27)

Passing on the Father's love

Conduct a library research project with your children about the history of Native Americans.

☐ Ash Wednesday _____

My dear children, I write this to you so that you will not sin. But if anybody does sin, we have one who speaks to the Father in our defense—Jesus Christ, the Righteous One. He is the atoning sacrifice for our sins, and not only for ours but also for the sins of the whole world. (1 John 2:1-2)

Passing on the Father's love

Attend an Ash Wednesday service in your community, or have a special family devotional time, concentrating on what it means that Jesus' death atoned for our sins.

☐ Easter _____

He is not here; he has risen, just as he said. (Matthew 28:6)

Passing on the Father's love

Attend a sunrise service or a church service together as a family.

☐ Election Day (1st Tuesday after 1st Monday in November)

Everyone must submit himself to the governing authorities, for there is no authority except that which God has established. The authorities that exist have been established by God. Consequently, he who rebels against the authority is rebelling against what God has instituted, and those who do so will bring judgment on themselves. (Romans 13:1-2)

Passing on the Father's love
Discuss political candidates, who your and your children's favorites are and why.

☐ Father's Day (3rd Sunday in June) _____

May the Lord continually bless you with Heaven's blessings as well as with human joys. May you live to enjoy your grandchildren! (Psalm 128:5-6, TLB)

Passing on the Father's love
Relax! Celebrate! You are the most important man in the world to your children.

☐ Flag Day (June 14) _____

[The Lord] will raise a banner for the nations and gather the exiles of Israel; he will assemble the scattered people of Judah from the four quarters of the earth. (Isaiah 11:12)

Passing on the Father's love
Have your kids help you display the flag at your house.

☐ Good Friday _____

This is how we know what love is: Jesus Christ laid down his life for us. And we ought to lay down our lives for our brothers. (1 John 3:16)

Passing on the Father's love
Ask your children why people call today "Good" Friday.

☐ Grandparents' Day (September) _____

Enter into His gates with thanksgiving, and into His courts with praise. Be thankful to Him, and bless His name. For the Lord is good; his mercy is everlasting and His truth endures to all generations. (Psalm 100:4-5, NKJV)

Passing on the Father's love

Help the children find a specific thing to do that will communicate their appreciation to their grandparents—a special homemade gift or card, an outing, etc.

☐ Independence Day (July 4) _____

It is God's will that by doing good you should silence the ignorant talk of foolish men. Live as free men, but do not use your freedom as a cover-up for evil; live as servants of God. Show proper respect to everyone: Love the brotherhood of believers, fear God, honor the king. (1 Peter 2:15-17)

Passing on the Father's love

Take your kids to see the fireworks. Enjoy them together. *Ooh* and *aah* at the big ones.

☐ Labor Day (1st Monday in September) _____

Unless the Lord builds the house, its builders labor in vain. . . . In vain you rise early and stay up late, toiling for food to eat—for he grants sleep to those he loves. (Psalm 127:1-2)

Passing on the Father's love
Enjoy your day off. Be proud that you work to provide for your family's needs.

☐ Lent (season) _____

Surely he took up our infirmities and carried our sorrows, yet we considered him stricken by God, smitten by him, and afflicted. But he was pierced for our transgressions, he was crushed for our iniquities; the punishment that brought us peace was upon him, and by his wounds we are healed. We all, like sheep, have gone astray, each of us has turned to his own way; and the Lord has laid on him the iniquity of us all. (Isaiah 53:4-6)

Passing on the Father's love
Choose as a family some way of demonstrating an attitude of repentance toward God during the Lenten season.

☐ Lincoln's Birthday (February 12) _____

I pray also for those who will believe in me through their message, that all of them may be one, Father, just as you are in me and I am in you. . . . May they be brought to complete unity to let the world know that you sent me and have loved them even as you have loved me. (John 17:20, 23)

Passing on the Father's love
Read the Gettysburg Address to your kids.

☐ Martin Luther King Jr. Day (January) _____

Both the one who makes men holy and those who are made holy are of the same family. So Jesus is not ashamed to call them brothers. (Hebrews 2:11)

Passing on the Father's love
Encourage your children to develop interracial friendships.

☐ Memorial Day (May 30) _____

Your sons will take the place of your fathers; you will make them princes throughout the land. (Psalm 45:16)

Passing on the Father's love
Visit a cemetery today, and tell your children about their ancestors.

☐ Mother's Day (2nd Sunday in May) _____

As a mother comforts her child, so will I comfort you; and you will be comforted over Jerusalem. (Isaiah 66:13)

Passing on the Father's love
Tell your wife the one thing that impresses you the most about her as the mother of your children.

☐ National Day of Prayer (1st Thursday in May) _____

If my people, who are called by my name, will humble themselves and pray and seek my face and turn from their wicked ways, then will I hear from heaven and will forgive their sin and will heal their land. (2 Chronicles 7:14)

Passing on the Father's love

Tell your kids that children across the country are praying for the nation today. Pray with them.

☐ Palm Sunday _____

Blessed is the king who comes in the name of the Lord! Peace in heaven and glory in the highest! (Luke 19:38)

Passing on the Father's love

To guarantee that your children have more than just a secular commemoration of Easter, begin today to celebrate the entire week of Christ's passion.

☐ Pentecost Sunday _____

All this I have spoken while still with you. But the Counselor, the Holy Spirit, whom the Father will send in my name, will teach you all things and will remind you of everything I have said to you. Peace I leave with you; my peace I give you. I do not give to you as the world gives. Do not let your hearts be troubled and do not be afraid. (John 14:25-27)

Passing on the Father's love

Ask your children what they think the Holy Spirit does in our lives.

☐ St. Patrick's Day (March 17) _____

A cheerful heart is good medicine. (Proverbs 17:22)

Passing on the Father's love
Pinch anyone in your family who isn't wearing green.

☐ Thanksgiving (4th Thursday in November) _____

Then Moses and the Israelites sang this song to the Lord: " . . . The Lord is my strength and my song; he has become my salvation. He is my God, and I will praise him, my father's God, and I will exalt him." (Exodus 15:1-2)

Passing on the Father's love
Place five kernels of corn at each plate. In a round-robin fashion, share one thing you are thankful for, using each kernel.

☐ Valentine's Day (February 14) _____

Enjoy life with the woman whom you love all the days of your fleeting life which He has given to you under the sun; for this is your reward in life, and in your toil in which you have labored under the sun. (Ecclesiastes 9:9, NASB)

Passing on the Father's love
Splurge on your wife tonight! Get a baby-sitter for the kids, take your wife out to dinner, and overwhelm her with romance.

☐ Veterans Day (November 11) _____

The Lord is the strength of his people, a fortress of salvation for his anointed one. Save your people and bless your inheritance; be their shepherd and carry them forever. (Psalm 28:8-9)

Passing on the Father's love
Tell your kids about your experience or that of a parent or grandparent who served in one of the wars.

☐ Washington's Birthday (February 22) _____

For dominion belongs to the Lord and he rules over the nations. (Psalm 22:28)

Passing on the Father's love
Ask your children why George Washington is called the father of our nation.